# The Beaut and Sala

*plant-based raw soup and salad recipes*

*by*

**Kachina Choate**
Summer Bear

Pistachio Tabbouleh Salad (page 45)

*Beautiful Soup: plant-based raw salad and soup recipes*

Copyright © 2020 Kachina Choate

First Edition 2020

ISBN (print) 978-1-938142-08-6
ISBN (eBook) 978-1-938142-09-3

1. Raw Foods 2. Cookery (Natural foods) 3. Soups 4. Salads

This book does not intend to cure or give medical advice. We want to educate, inform, and empower readers to make their own decisions on their health and well-being. Each person might have different reactions to changes in diet. If you have concerns about your health or nutrition, consult your health-care advisor.

# Table of Contents

Taco Salad (page 63)

# Introduction

Soups and salads are a part of many meals, and if you are planning a multi course dinner at least one will be served if not both. Traditionally soup is served as the first course, salads the forth or eighth course depending on how many courses in the complete meal.

When soup is used as a first course the rest of the meal should be kept in mind. If the meal is hearty and rich, a clear soup is a good start. If the meal is on the lighter side then a rich creamy soup is a good choice.

Salads are classified by when they served within a meal, appetizer salad served as a first course. Dinner salad, served with the main course. The entrée salad or main dish is the main course in a meal.

Not only are salads classified by when they are served but how they are made.

**Green salad** includes leafy vegetables and garnishes. **Vegetable salad** ingredients can include onions carrots, celery, radishes, peppers, tomatoes, and cucumbers they may or may not contain greens. **Bound Salads** include thick sauces and are often used as sandwich fillings. Main dish or **entrée salads** are standalone salad and often contain protein. **Fruit salads** are made from fruits and dessert salads contained whipped cream or other sweet foods.

Salads can be composed salad, where the salad is arranged on a plate or tossed salad where the vegetables are mixed in a bowl.

While not many people will eat, an eleven-course meal most will eat a three-course meal where the first course is a salad followed by entrée and finished off with a dessert.

---

"Food is not just calories, it is information. It talks to your DNA and tell it what to do. The most powerful tool to change your health, environment and entire world is your fork."

– Dr. Mark Hyman

# Kale Soup

*Preparation:*  *Makes 4-6*
*45 Min.*   *Servings*

## Ingredients

- 1 onion
- 1 clove garlic
- ¼ tsp. red pepper flakes
- 1 ½ c. jicama, peeled and cubed
- 1 bunch kale, with stem removed
- 3 c. vegetable base (page 26)
- kale microgreens, garish

## Directions

Make vegetable base. Remove stems from kale and tear into bite-sized pieces.

Peel jicama then cut into ¼ inch cubes. Place jicama in a bowl along with onion, garlic, kale, red pepper flakes, and vegetable base blend until smooth.

Garnish with kale microgreens.

# Mexican Vegetable Soup

Preparation:    Drying:    Makes 4-6
30 Min.      1-3 Hrs.    Servings

## Ingredients

- 1 tbsp. cold pressed olive oil
- ½ yellow or orange bell pepper, diced
- 1 red bell pepper, diced
- 1 tbsp. ground cumin
- ½ tsp. dried oregano
- ¼ tsp. cayenne pepper
- 1 tomatoes, diced
- 1 tbsp. jalapeno pepper, diced
- 2 c. vegetable soup base (page 26)
- 1 c. corn kernels
- 1 zucchini, diced
- Himalayan crystal salt
- pepper to taste

### Optional Toppings

- lime juice
- avocado
- cilantro
- sour cream (page 113)

## Directions

Make vegetable base and set aside. In a bowl, place bell peppers, jalapeno, zucchini, corn, salt, cumin, oregano, cayenne pepper, and pepper.

Pour vegetable base over vegetable and stir. Place in dehydrator for about 1-3 hours to warm if desired. Add tomatoes and any optional toppings. Serve immediately.

---

"'Beautiful Soup, so rich and green, ...
Who for such dainties would not stoop?
Soup of the evening, beautiful Soup! "
–Lewis Carroll,
'Alice in Wonderland'

# Red Pepper Tomato Soup

*Preparation:*  *Makes*
*15 Min.*  *4-6Servings*

## Ingredients

- 1 tbsp. cold pressed olive oil (optional)
- ½ c. dried tomatoes, soaked 15 minutes in pure water
- 1 onion, chopped
- 1 clove garlic
- 3 red bell peppers
- 4 large tomatoes
- 1 ½ tsp. dried thyme
- 2 tsp. paprika
- 1 pinch ground cayenne pepper
- Himalayan crystal salt to taste
- pepper to taste
- sour cream, (page 113, optional garnish)

## Directions

Soak dried tomatoes for at least 15 minutes in just enough pure water to cover. Place tomatoes in a blender with the water.

Wash and cut fresh tomatoes then place in blender with olive oil.

Cut and seed bell peppers add to the blender along with chopped onion, garlic, thyme, paprika, cayenne pepper, salt, and pepper then blend until smooth.

Warm if desired. Place in soup bowls and garnish with sour cream and/or tomato and red pepper slices just before serving.

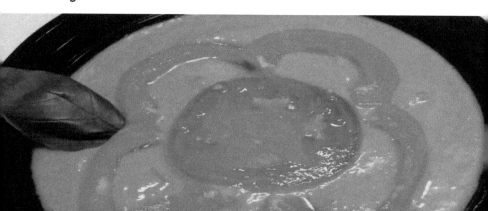

# Creamy Curried Cauliflower Soup

*Preparation:* 25 Min.  *Drying:* 2-4 Hrs.  *Makes 2-4 Servings*

## Ingredients

- ¼ c. sunflower seeds
- 3 ½ c. almond milk (page 114)
- 5 tsp. mild curry powder
- 1 c. chopped yellow onion
- 3 cloves garlic
- 5 c. cauliflower florets
- Himalayan crystal salt to taste
- white pepper to taste

## Directions

Soak sunflower seeds overnight, drain off the water. Mix seeds with 1 tsp. curry powder and place in dehydrator for about 24 hours, mixing them at least once.

In a blender, place cauliflower, garlic, onion, 4 tsp. curry powder, and almond milk. Combine until smooth. Taste and season with Himalayan salt and white pepper

Transfer to serving bowl, garnish with dried sunflower seeds and serve.

# Cream of Cauliflower Soup

Preparation: 20 Min.  Makes 2-4 Servings

## Ingredients

- 1 head cauliflower
- 1 carrot, shredded
- 2 stocks celery
- 1 c. cashews
- ¼ c. olive oil
- 1 tsp. turmeric
- 1 tsp. Himalayan crystal salt
- ¼ tsp. pepper
- 1 c. young coconut, meat and water
- dash paprika

## Directions

Wash and chop cauliflower, save ¼ c. for garnish.

Place the remaining cauliflower in a blender add carrot, celery, cashews, young coconut meat, oil, turmeric, coconut water, salt, and pepper and blend until creamy.

Place in bowl and garnish with the reserved cauliflower and sprinkle with paprika.

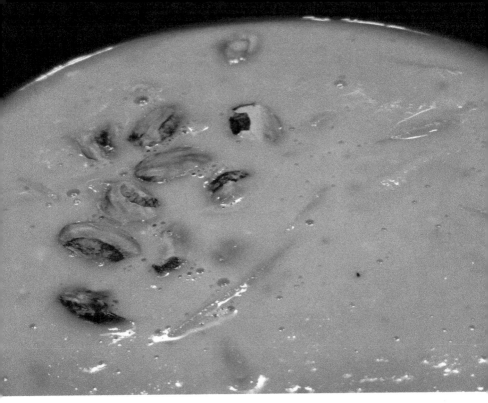

# Curried Carrot Soup with Pistachios

*Preparation: 15 Min.*   *Makes 4-6 Servings*

## Ingredients

- 2 tbsp. cold pressed olive oil
- 4 c. carrots, grated
- 1 leek, thinly sliced
- ½ tsp. curry powder
- ¼ c. pistachios, shelled
- Himalayan crystal salt to taste

## Directions

Thinly slice and wash leek. Place leek in a blender with olive oil.

Grate carrots and place in blender with curry powder and salt blend until creamy adding water as needed.

Pour soup in serving bowls. Divide pistachios equally between bowls and place in the center.

# Vegetable "Noodle" Soup

*Preparation:* *Makes 4-6*
*30 Min.* *Servings*

## Soup Base

## Ingredients

- 2 c. pure water
- 2 tsp. cold pressed olive oil
- ½ c. celery
- ½ c. onion
- ¼ tsp. poultry seasoning
- 2 tsp. Himalayan crystal salt
- ½ tsp. white pepper

## "Noodles"

- ½ c. celery, sliced
- 1 c. carrot
- 1 c. zucchini
- ½ c. broccoli

## Directions

In a blender, combine celery, onion, poultry seasoning, salt, pepper, and oil until smooth. Adding enough water to make it the texture and thickness you desire. Set aside.

Prepare noodles by thinly slicing celery and carrots. Chop broccoli then place in a bowl with celery and carrots. Make zucchini noodles using a spiralizer or shred. Cut zucchini into shorter strips add to the bowl.

Cover ingredients in bowl with blended soup base. Add more salt and pepper if desired.

---

**Fun Fact:**

This soup is a good substitute for chicken noodle soup when you are not feeling well.

---

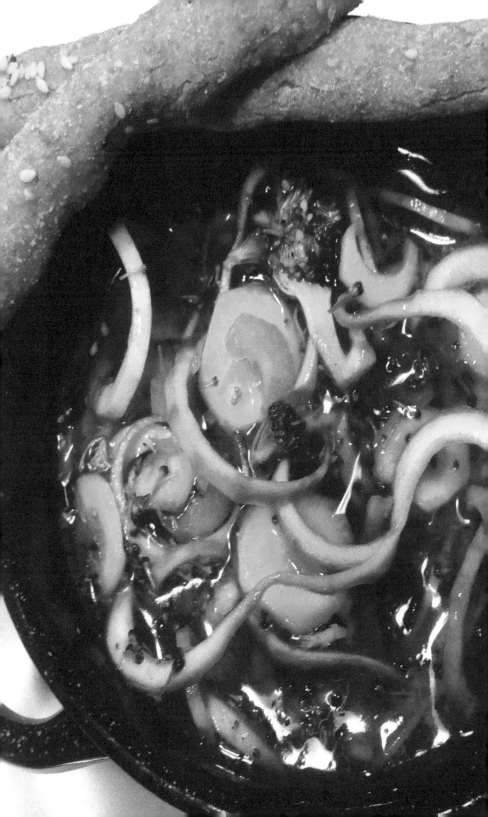

# Jicama and Olive Soup

Preparation:   Soaking:   Makes 4-6
25 Min.   8-12 Hrs   Servings

## Ingredients

- ¼ c. medium onion
- 4 tbsp. cold pressed olive oil
- 4 c. jicama
- 1 sprigs fresh thyme
- ¼ c. sun dried olives
- ½ tsp. Himalayan crystal salt
- ½ c. pumpkin seeds, soaked overnight
- 1 lemon, juiced
- 1 tbsp. Italian seasoning

## Directions

Soak pumpkin seeds overnight. Drain the water off.

Peel and grate jicama. Set aside 1 cup for floaters. Place the rest in a blender with onion, olive oil, thyme, salt, pumpkin seeds, lemon juice and Italian seasoning. Blend until creamy, add pumpkin seeds and mix.

Pour soup in serving bowls then place reserved jicama and olives in the middle.

# End of Summer Soup

Preparation: Makes 2-4
20 Min.      Servings

## Ingredients

- 2 c. turnips or jicama
- ¾ c. peas
- ½ c. carrots
- 1 green onion
- 1 ¼ c. cashew or almond milk (page 114)
- 1 tbsp. cold pressed olive oil (optional)
- ¼ tsp. turmeric
- 1 tsp. Himalayan crystal salt
- ½ tsp. white pepper

## Directions

Peel and chop turnip or jicama into bite sized pieces.

Thinly slice carrots and place in a bowl with 1 cup turnip/jicama. Add peas to the bowl and mix.

In a blender, combine remaining turnip/jicama, nut milk, green onion, turmeric, salt, white pepper, and oil. Pour the blended ingredients over the vegetables and serve.

15

# Cool Cucumber Soup

Preparation: Makes 2-4
10 Min.      Servings

## Ingredients

- 2 medium cucumbers
- ½ small onion
- 3 celery stocks, cut into ½ inch pieces
- 1 tbsp. lemon juice or raw apple cider vinegar
- 2 tsp. Himalayan crystal salt
- water as needed
- garnish: parsley

## Directions

Blend cucumbers, onion, celery, lemon juice, and salt in a blender until smooth. Adding only enough water to achieve desired thickness.

Garnish soup with parsley.

# Ginger Turmeric Carrot Soup

Preparation:    Chill:    Makes 4-6
25 Min.    2-8 Hrs.    Servings

## Ingredients

- 1 tbsp. coconut oil
- 1 green onions, copped
- 1 clove garlic
- ½ inch ginger, peeled
- pinch cayenne pepper
- 2 carrots, sliced
- ½ tsp. Himalayan crystal salt
- ½ tsp. black pepper
- ¼ tsp. cinnamon
- ½ tsp. turmeric
- ¼ - 1 c. water

## Directions

In a blender, combine coconut oil, green onion, garlic, ginger, cayenne, carrot, salt, pepper, cinnamon, and turmeric mix. Add only enough water to achieve desired thickness.

# Gazpacho

*Preparation: Makes 6-8*
*25 Min.    Servings*

## Ingredients

- 3 c. tomatoes, chopped
- 1 lime, juiced
- 1 clove garlic
- ½ c. cucumber, chopped
- ½ jalapeno pepper, seeded and chopped
- 2 green onions, chopped
- 1 red bell peppers, chopped
- 1 tsp. Himalayan crystal salt
- ½ tsp. cumin, ground
- ¼ tsp. black pepper
- 1 tbsp. fresh basil leaves
- 1 tbsp. cold pressed olive oil (optional)

## Directions

In a large mixing bowl place chopped tomatoes, cucumber, and bell peppers then stir to combine. Transfer 1 ½ cups of the mixture to a blender.

To tomato mixture in blender add garlic, cumin, black pepper, jalapeno, green onion, lime juice, olive oil, and salt then purée. Return puréed mixture to the bowl and stir to combine.

Cover and chill for at least 2 hours. Garnish with basil before serving.

---

**Fun Fact:**

Gazpacho is a soup made of raw vegetables and served cold. There are many theories about the origin of this soup but all agree that it has ancient roots.

The internationally known red gazpacho with tomatoes evolved in the 19th century. However, today it can vary with different colors and ingredients.

It is a refreshing meal eaten during the hot summer and very popular in Spain and Portugal.

---

# Rabbits Carrot Soup

Preparation: Makes 4-6
25 Min.     Servings

## Ingredients

- 4 c. carrots, shredded
- 2 celery stalks, chopped
- 1 c. cashews or macadamia nuts
- 2 tsp. cold pressed olive oil
- ¼ c. onion, chopped
- 2 cloves garlic, chopped
- 2 lemons, juiced
- pinch ginger
- water as needed
- Himalayan crystal salt to taste
- pepper to taste

## Directions

In a large bowl, place 2 cups of shredded carrots. Set aside.

In a blender, combine remaining carrots, celery, cashews, olive oil, onion, garlic, lemon juice, ginger, salt, and pepper adding water to achieve the desired thickness.

Pour the blender ingredients over reserved carrots.

# Broccoli Soup

*Preparation:*   *Makes 2-4*
*15 Min.*     *Servings*

## Ingredients

- 1-2 tsp. cold pressed olive oil
- 1 clove garlic, minced
- ¼ cup onion, minced
- 1 c. cashews
- 2-4 c. water
- 2-4 c. broccoli
- 2 tbsp. parsley
- Himalayan crystal salt to taste
- 1 lemon, juiced
- 2 celery stalks, thinly sliced
- 1 c. cherry tomatoes
- 1 avocado, cubed
- 1 tsp. kelp

## Directions

In a blender, purée cashews, onion, garlic, olive oil, broccoli, parsley, and lemon juice add water as needed. Blend until smooth and the desired consistency is achieved.

I like to have floaters in my soups; there are many different kinds for this soup. You can cube avocado, sliced celery, or broccoli floweret.

Pour purée into a bowl and place the floaters on top just before serving.

# Leek Soup

Preparation: Makes 4-6
25 Min.      Servings

## Ingredients

- 3 bay leaves
- 12 peppercorns
- 10 fresh parsley stems
- 1 sprig fresh thyme
- 1 clove garlic
- 1 leek, thinly sliced
- 4 c. vegetable base (page 26)
- ½ tsp. Himalayan crystal salt
- ¼ c. micro greens
- 1 tsp. lemon zest
- ¼ c. celery, sliced
- ¼ c. jicama, cubed
- ½ micro greens

## Directions

Make vegetable base and place in a bowl. Place bay leaves, peppercorn, parsley and thyme in a piece of cheesecloth and tie up the ends. Place cheesecloth packet in bowl with vegetable base. Let it set overnight.

In a bowl, place thinly sliced leek, celery, and jicama.

Remove the cheesecloth packet from base. Pour base over the leeks. Garnish with micro greens and serve.

# Fresh Garden Soup

Preparation: 30 Min.   Makes 4-6 Servings

## Ingredients

- 3 green onions, chopped
- 1 c. turnip, diced
- 1 c. carrots, thinly sliced
- 1 c. celery, thinly sliced
- 1 c. zucchini, chopped
- 1 c. summer yellow squash, chopped
- 1 c. cabbage, shredded
- 4 c. tomatoes
- ½ tsp. Himalayan crystal salt
- ½ tsp. black pepper
- ½ tsp. basil
- ½ tsp. oregano
- ½ tsp. rosemary
- 2 cloves garlic, pressed
- 2 tsp. cold pressed olive oil

## Directions

Chop green onion, turnip, zucchini, and yellow squash then place in a bowl. To the bowl add shredded cabbage, thinly slice carrots, and celery toss .

Place tomatoes in a blender add salt, pepper, basil, oregano, rosemary, garlic, and olive oil then blend until well mixed.

Pour tomato mixture over vegetables. May warm to 100° F.

---

**Fun Facts:**

Summer squash originates from Mexico and Central America. Scientists have found summer squash seeds preserved in Mexican caves that are over 10,000 years old. They are available in several different varieties. Each variety has a unique shape, color, size and flavor

# Enchilada Soup

*Preparation:* *Makes 4-6*
*25 Min.* *Servings*

## Ingredients

- 6 Anaheim peppers
- 1 tbsp. cold pressed olive oil
- ½ c. onion, chopped
- 1-2 clove garlic
- 1 c. hazelnuts, soaked
- 4 c. tomatoes, chopped
- 1 red bell pepper, chopped
- ¼ c. dried tomatoes
- 1 tsp. cumin seed, ground
- 2 tsp. oregano
- ¾ tsp. paprika
- black pepper to taste
- 1 tsp. Himalayan crystal salt
- ½ c. sundried olives, sliced (optional)
- ½ c. scallions, sliced
- ¾ c. almond sour cream (page 113)

## Directions

Soak hazelnuts overnight and drain water off nuts then chop. Remove stems and seeds from peppers.

In a blender, combine Anaheim peppers, onion, olive oil garlic, cumin, oregano, paprika, black pepper, dried, tomatoes, and salt then purée until smooth adding more water if needed.

Place hazelnuts, tomatoes, and red bell pepper in bowl. Pour blender mix over tomatoes and let marinate for at least an hour. Warm to 100° F before serving. Garnish with sour cream, sliced scallions and olives.

> **Fun Facts:**
>
> In the Middle ages it was believed that cumin kept chickens and lovers from running away!
>
> It was also said that if cumin was carried during a wedding happiness would follow.

# Vegetable Base

*Preparation:*   *Makes 4-6*
*10 Min.*      *Servings*

## Ingredients

- ½ c. onion
- 1 c. turnip
- 1 c. parsnip
- 8 c. celery
- 1 zucchini, diced
- Himalayan crystal salt
- pepper to taste
- 1-3 c. water

## Directions

Combine onion, carrots, turnip, parsnip, and celery in a blender. Add water as needed to achieve a thin mixture.

Pour mixture into milk bag or a clean nylon knee high and strain over a bowl.

Squeeze to make sure all the liquid is out. Add salt and pepper to juice and let set for at least an hour.

## Note

The leftover vegetable pulp is a good start for raw crackers. Just add soaked nuts and or seeds, seasoning and any other vegetables, then dry in dehydrator.

## Variation

For a more traditional vegetable base place washed peels and ends of organic vegetables (zucchini, parsnips, turnips, celery, lettuce, lemon, carrots, and other root type vegetables) not used in other recipes and place them in a bowl with warm water.

Add salt, pepper, thyme, bay leaf, and any other spices you enjoy. Stir the spices and vegetable peels.

Cover bowl and set on counter or in the sun for a few days. Taste the water when the flavor is what you enjoy, strain though a sieve, save the liquid (soup base) and compost the vegetable peels.

# Taco Soup

Preparation: 25 Min.  Soaking: 8-12 Hrs.  Makes 4-6 Servings

## Ingredients

- 1 c. hazelnuts, soaked
- 1 c. corn, fresh or frozen
- 5 tomatoes, chopped fresh
- ½ cup dried tomatoes,
- ½ onion, chopped
- 1 tbsp. cold pressed olive oil
- 1 tsp. garlic Powder
- Mexican spice to taste
- Himalayan crystal salt to taste
- pepper to taste
- 2 c. pure water as needed

## Directions

Soak hazelnuts overnight. Drain off the water and roughly chop nuts. Set aside.

Soak dried tomatoes in pure water for 15 minutes. Place dried tomatoes with soaking water, olive oil, onion, 2 of the tomatoes, garlic, Mexican or taco seasoning, salt, and pepper to taste in a blender and purée.

Cut kernels of the corn, if fresh is unavailable you can use frozen. Chop 3 of the fresh tomatoes and place in a bowl with the corn, add hazelnuts and pour the blender ingredients over the top. Gently mix. May warm to 100° F if desired. Garnish with sliced avocadoes or guacamole.

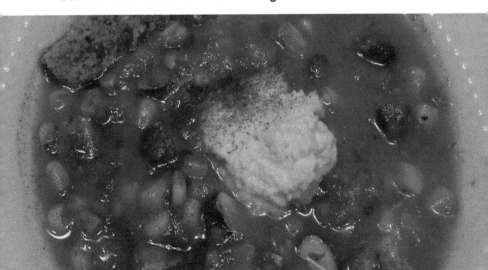

# Italian Tomato Soup

Preparation: 20 Min.   Makes 4-6 Servings

## Ingredients

- 1 c. dried tomatoes
- 6 fresh tomatoes
- ½ tbsp. Italian seasoning
- 2-3 green onions
- 1-2 zucchinis
- 2-4 cloves garlic
- 3 tbsp. cold pressed olive oil (optional)
- Himalayan crystal salt to taste
- pepper to taste
- sunflower greens, for garnish (optional)

## Directions

Soak dried tomatoes in water for 15 minutes and place in a blender. Add fresh tomatoes, green onions, zucchini, yellow squash, garlic, olive oil, salt, and pepper blend until smooth.

Place in soup bowls and garnish with sunflower greens and/or cherry tomatoes.

# Sprouted Soup

Preparation:    Sprouting:    Makes 4-6
15 Min.      1-3 Days.    Servings

## Ingredients

- ¼ c. adzuki beans, sprouted
- ¼ c. fenugreek, sprouted
- ¼ c. lentils, sprouted
- ¼ c. mung beans, sprouted
- ½ c. peas, sprouted
- 1 carrot, chopped
- 1 celery, chopped
- ¼ - ½ c. onion, chopped
- 1 clove garlic
- 1 red bell pepper, chopped
- 2 tomatoes, chopped
- Himalayan crystal salt to taste
- 2 ½ tsp. poultry seasoning
- 1 ½ c. pure water
- 1 tbsp. cold pressed olive oil (optional)

## Directions

Sprout fenugreek, lentils, green peas, peas, adzuki and mung beans.

Wash and chop onion, carrots, bell peppers, tomatoes, celery, and garlic place in a bowl. Add spouts and toss.

In a small bowl, place water, oil, salt, and poultry seasoning and mix or use vegetable base (page 26). Pour over spouts and vegetables.

# Apple Parsnip Soup

## Ingredients

- 2 tbsp. cold pressed olive oil
- 2 green onions, chopped
- 5 celery stocks, sliced
- 5 medium apples, chopped
- 4 parsnips
- 1 tsp. parsley
- ¼ c. cashews or macadamia nuts
- water as needed
- Himalayan crystal salt to taste
- pepper to taste

## Directions

Cut and soak parsnips in water overnight in refrigerator.

In a blender, combine cold pressed olive oil, green onions, 3 stalks of celery, 3 apples, parsnips, and nuts until smooth. Add only enough water to obtain desired thickness.

Chop 2 apples and slice 2 stalks of celery then place in a bowl and cover with blended ingredients.

---

### Fun Fact:

Parsnips have been cultivated for their sweet roots since ancient times. Its early history is clouded because writers didn't always distinguish them from carrots. Parsnips look pretty much like beige carrots with really wide shoulders. Roman Emperor Tiberius was picky about parsnips. He had wild ones specially imported from the banks of the Rhine, the colder climate allowed the roots to develop a sweeter flavor.

Parsnips were of supreme importance in the medieval European kitchen. Sugar was a rare, imported luxury, and honey could be expensive so the sweet, starchy parsnip did double duty for the cook—besides serving as a vegetable, it could be used to sweeten and thicken various puddings. When sugar became cheap in Europe, the parsnip's popularity waned.

---

# Hearty Vegetable Soup

*Preparation: Makes 6-8*
*10 Min.     Servings*

## Ingredients

- 1 c. vegetable base (page 26)
- 2 ½ c. zucchini, chopped
- 4 fresh tomatoes, chopped
- 2 c. green cabbage, chopped
- 1 c. celery, sliced
- 1 c. carrots, sliced
- 1 c. red bell pepper, chopped
- ¼ c. green onions, sliced
- ¼ c. fresh parsley, chopped
- 1 clove garlic
- ¾ c. corn kernels
- ¾ c. green beans, cut
- Himalayan crystal salt to taste
- pepper to taste
- ½ c. mushrooms, sliced (optional)

## Directions

Prepare vegetable base and set aside.

In a blender, purée half a zucchini, one tomato, ¼ cup corn kernels, green onions, vegetable base, parsley, garlic, salt, and pepper.

Chop cabbage, onion, bell pepper, parsley, zucchinis and tomatoes place in a bowl. Thinly slice carrots, mushrooms, and celery then add to cabbage bowl add corn and mix.

Pour blender purée over vegetables. Warm if desired.

---

**Fun Fact:**

The key to making soups is to have a great base. Soup base is the culmination of layering of flavors Something that can be made into any flavor pallet.

---

# Corn and Chili Pepper Soup

*Preparation:* *Makes 4-6*
*15 Min.* *Servings*

## Ingredients

**Soup**

- 1 chili pepper
- ½ c. almond milk (page 114)
- 1 clove garlic
- 1 lime, juiced
- ½ tsp. Himalayan crystal Salt
- ¼ tsp. cumin, ground
- 2 tbsp. cold pressed olive oil
- ½ c. onion, thinly sliced
- ¼ tsp. coriander, ground
- 3 c. corn, cornels off the cob

**Avocado Relish**

- ½ c. radishes, diced
- ½ avocado
- 2 tsp. lime, juiced

## Directions

In a blender place chili pepper, almond milk, garlic, vinegar, salt, cumin, olive oil, onion, coriander, and 2 ½ cups of corn mix until creamy.

Dice radishes and pace in a bowl. Juice lime and place in a bowl with radishes. Peel and dice avocado and combine with radishes and the reaming ½ cup corn.

Divide vegetables into serving bowls and pour blender mixture over top. Divide relish and place equal amounts on top of the soup.

> **Fun Fact:**
>
> In the days of the early settlers to North America corn was so valuable that it was used as money.

# Jalapeno Soup

*Preparation:* *Makes 4-6*
*15 Min.* *Servings*

## Ingredients

- 1 avocado, peeled and pitted
- ¼ c. yellow onion
- 1 clove garlic
- 1-2 jalapenos, depending on how hot they are
- 2 c. cauliflower
- 2 tbsp. parsley
- 2 lemons, juiced
- ¼ tsp. cumin
- ½ tsp. Himalayan crystal salt
- ½ tsp. black pepper
- ¾ c. water
- garnish: sour cream (page 113) and sliced jalapeno.

## Directions

In a blender combine peeled and pitted avocado, onion, garlic, jalapeno, cauliflower, parsley, lemon juice, cumin, water, salt, and black pepper until smooth.

Divide soup in serving bowls and garnish with almond sour cream and sliced jalapeno.

# Apple Pumpkin Soup

Preparation: Soaking: Makes 4-6
15 Min.    8-12 Hrs.   Servings

## Ingredients

- 4 c. pumpkin, peeled, seeded and cubed
- ½ c. cold pressed olive oil
- 2 green onions
- 4 stalks of celery, sliced
- 6 medium apples, chopped
- 1 tsp. parsley
- ¼ tsp. pumpkin pie spice
- water as needed
- Himalayan crystal salt to taste
- pepper to taste

## Directions

Chop 3 apples and thinly sliced 2 celery stalks place in a bowl and set aside.

In a blender, mix pumpkin, olive oil, green onion, 2 celery stalks, 3 apples, parsley, pumpkin pie spice, salt, and pepper until desired constancy is reached adding water as needed.

Pour blended soup over reserved apple and celery and enjoy.

---

### Fun Fact:

An apple a day may really keep the doctor away. Apples are low in calories and free of fat, sodium and cholesterol.

They are rich in fiber, disease fighting anti-oxidants and a variety of vitamins and minerals including potassium, folate, niacin, and vitamins A, B, C, E, and K.

Eating apples has been associated with lower risk of a variety of cancers, stroke and diabetes.

They may help protect the brain from developing Alzheimer's and Parkinson's disease, and even lower a person's risk of tooth decay.

---

# Pumpkin African Stew

*Preparation:* *Makes 6-8*
*30 Min.* *Servings*

## Ingredients

- 1 ½ c. pumpkin
- 1 clove garlic
- 1 ½ c. tomatoes
- 2 green onions
- 1 c. peas
- 1 lemon, juiced
- 1 young coconut
- 1 tsp. chili powder
- 1 tsp. turmeric
- ½ tsp. cumin
- ½ tsp. Himalayan crystal salt
- pepper to taste
- raw pumpkin seeds to garnish

## Directions

Peel, seed and cube pumpkin.

In blender, mix young coconut meat and coconut water with 1 cup pumpkin, garlic, green onion, lemon, turmeric, cumin, salt, pepper, and chili powder. Blend until smooth and creamy.

In a bowl, place remaining pumpkin, peas, and diced tomatoes. Pour creamy blender mix over the top. Garnish with pumpkin seeds.

# Pumpkin Chowder

*Preparation: 30 Min.*  *Makes 2-4 Servings*

## Ingredients

- ½ c. green onion, chopped
- 2 c. pumpkin, puréed
- 1 c. pumpkin seed milk (page 114)
- ½ c. peas
- ½ c. carrots
- ½ c. rutabaga or turnip
- 1 tsp. thyme
- 1 tsp. turmeric
- 1 tsp. pumpkin pie spice
- 1 tsp. ginger
- Himalayan crystal salt to taste

## Directions

Peel and chop pumpkin then place in a blender along with onion, oil, thyme, turmeric, pumpkin pie spice, and ginger blend until well mixed.

Add pumpkin seed milk slowly until desired thickness is achieved.

In a bowl place sliced carrots, rutabaga/turnip and peas. Pour blender mixture over vegetables, add salt and pepper to taste.

# Chili Stew

| Preparation: | Soaking: | Sprouting: | Makes 4-6 |
| 40 Min. | 20 Min. | 2-3 Days | Servings |

## Ingredients

- 1 c. adzuki beans, sprouted (optional)
- 2 c. fresh tomatoes, chopped
- 1 c. dried tomatoes, soaked in 3 cups of pure water
- 2 large red bell pepper, chopped
- 2 ¾ c. corn, fresh or frozen
- 1 medium zucchini, chopped
- 1 ½ c. mushrooms, ground
- 1 or 2 hot peppers, if desired
- 2 cloves garlic, minced
- 2 tbsp. cold pressed olive oil
- ¼ c. lemon or lime Juice
- ½ tsp. celery seed
- ½ tsp. chili powder or more to taste
- 1 ½ tsp. mustard seed, ground
- pinch cayenne pepper
- ¼ tsp. coriander, ground
- pure water to make desired thickness

## Directions

Sprout adzuki beans, until a small quarter inch or shorter tail appears.

Place sprouted adzuki beans, 1 ½ cups fresh tomatoes, 1 bell pepper, zucchini, mushrooms, and 2 cups of the corn in a bowl. Set aside.

In a blender mix dried tomatoes, ½ cup fresh tomatoes, 1 red pepper, ¾ cup corn, garlic, olive oil, lemon juice, celery seed, chili powder, mustard seed powder, cayenne pepper, and coriander until smooth.

Add enough water until the desired thickness is achieved. Pour over reserved vegetables. May warm to 100° F.

# Wild Rice Chowder

| Preparation: 25 Min. | Soaking: 8-12 Hrs. | Sprouting: 2-3 Days | Makes 4-6 Servings |
|---|---|---|---|

## Ingredients

- 2 tbsp. cold pressed olive oil
- 7 fresh mushrooms, sliced
- 1 stalk celery, thinly sliced
- 3 c. wild rice, sprouted
- 1 tsp. Himalayan crystal salt
- ½ tsp. mustard seed powder
- 1 small hot pepper, minced
- ½ c. Almonds, soaked overnight
- ½ tsp. onion powder
- ½ tsp. poultry seasoning
- pepper to taste
- pinch of paprika

## Directions

Sprout or bloom wild rice in water for 1-3 days, changing water every day. Rice may split down the middle and that is okay. Drain off water and set rice aside.

Soak almonds overnight and drain water off and place almonds in a blender.

To blender add olive oil, mushrooms, half the celery, 2 cups wild rice, hot pepper, onion, poultry seasoning, pepper, and paprika blend until smooth and creamy. Add water if needed to make it smooth and creamy.

Gently mix in remaining rice and celery for a nice crunch to the chowder. May warm this to 100°F.

Serve as a chowder or over shredded cabbage or zucchini.

## Note

1) For a dark colored chowder, use a Portobello or brown mushroom; for a lighter colored chowder use the light colored button mushrooms

2) For a gravy or a smooth chowder blend all ingredients until smooth.

# Parsnip Chowder

Preparation: Makes 2-4
30 Min.    Servings

## Ingredients

- 1 c. carrots, diced
- 1 c. jicama, diced
- 2 c. parsnips, diced
- 1 ½ c. onion, diced
- 1 ½ c. water
- ¾ c. cashews
- 1 tsp. Himalayan crystal salt
- ½ tsp. white pepper
- 1 tbsp. cold pressed olive oil
- ½ tsp. turmeric

## Directions

Peel and dice parsnips, carrots, and jicama then place in a bowl.

In a blender, combine cashews, onion, oil, salt, pepper, and turmeric, blend until smooth. If it is too thin, add more cashews.

Pour blender mix over the vegetables and serve.

# Corn Chowder

*Preparation:*   *Makes 4-6*
  *20 Min.*     *Servings*

## Ingredients

- 1 tbsp. cold pressed olive oil
- ½ c. green onion, chopped
- 2 c. corn
- 1 c. nut or seed milk (page 114)
- ½ c. celery, thinly sliced
- ½ c. carrots, thinly sliced
- ½ c. rutabaga or turnip, diced
- ¼ c. red bell pepper, diced
- ¼ c. broccoli floweret, diced
- ¼ tsp. thyme
- ¼ tsp. turmeric

## Directions

Place 1 cup of corn, onion, olive oil, thyme, and turmeric in blender and purée until well mixed. Slowly add pumpkin seed milk until the desired thickness is achieved.

Slice celery, carrots, red bell pepper, broccoli, and rutabaga place in serving bowls with reaming corn. Pour purée over the vegetables. Add salt and pepper to taste.

# Watermelon Soup

Preparation:    Chill:    Makes 6-8
20 Min.    60 Min.    Servings

## Ingredients

- 5 c. watermelon, cut and seeded
- 1 ½ c. raw cashews
- 3 zucchinis, cut into pieces
- ¼ c. raw liquid sweetener
- 2 tbsp. mint, chopped finely
- 1 pint berries (strawberries, blackberries)
- water if needed

## Directions

Purée watermelon in a blender, this may need to be done in batches. Pour watermelon purée in a bowl and set aside.

In a blender, mix cashews, raw liquid sweetener, and one tablespoon mint until creamy add water, as needed. It should look like a thick cream.

Place berries in the bowl with watermelon, add cashew mixture, and remaining mint gently mix. Garnish with a whole mint leaf and berries.

# Sweet Summer Soup

Preparation: Makes 4-6
25 Min.     Servings

## Ingredients

### Base

- ½ c. macadamia nuts
- ½ tsp. vanilla
- ½ c. pure water
- 1 orange
- 1 tsp. mint
- ½ tsp. cinnamon, ground

### Fruit

- 1 c. strawberries
- 1 c. cantaloupe
- 1 c. orange
- 1 c. pineapple
- 1 c. honeydew

## Directions

Place peeled orange in a blender. Add macadamia nuts, vanilla, mint, cinnamon and water, blend until smooth. Chill while preparing fruit.

In a bowl, prepare and place sliced strawberries, chopped cantaloupe, orange, pineapple, and honeydew.

Pour macadamia nut mixture over fruit and gently mix. Chill at least 2 hours. Garnish with orange segments and mint.

"To make a good salad is to be a brilliant diplomatist - the problem is entirely the same in both cases. To know how much oil one must mix with one's vinegar."

-Oscar Wilde'

# Pistachio Tabbouleh Salad

*Preparation:* *Makes 2-4*
*20 Min.* *Servings*

## Ingredients

- 2 c. hemp seeds, soaked overnight
- 1 c. cucumber, chopped
- 2 green onions, finely chopped
- 1 c. raw pistachio nuts, chopped
- ½ c. parsley, fresh and chopped
- ¼ c. lime, juiced
- 2 tbsp. mint, fresh and chopped
- 1 tbsp. cold pressed olive oil (optional)
- ½ tsp. Himalayan crystal salt

## Directions

Soak hemp seeds overnight, drain off water and place hemp in a bowl.

To the bowl add chopped pistachio, cucumber, green onion, parsley, mint, lime juice, olive oil, and salt mix with hemp seeds.

Cover bowl and refrigerate at least 1 hour before serving for flavors to mingle.

## Variation

Use sprouted quinoa in place of hemp seeds.

### Fun Facts

In China pistachios are known as "happy nut" and in Iran they are the "smiling nut" they also known as the "green almond".

# Moroccan Buckwheat Salad

*Preparation:*    *Soaking*    *Makes 2-4*
*15 Min.*    *8-12 Hrs.*    *Servings*

## Ingredients

- 1 c. buckwheat groats, soaked
- handful kale
- ½ c. carrots
- 1 avocado
- 1 lemon, juiced
- 1 c. zucchini, chopped
- ½ c. cashews (optional)
- 1 tsp. cinnamon
- 1 tsp. allspice
- ¼ c. fresh mint, chopped
- ½ tsp. Himalayan crystal salt
- pepper to taste
- 1 tsp. cold pressed olive oil

## Directions

Soak buckwheat overnight. Drain off water and rinse then place buckwheat into a bowl.

Wash kale, remove the steam, tear kale into small pieces, and add to the bowl with buckwheat.

Chop mint, shred carrots, slice zucchini and cube avocados then toss with buckwheat, kale and cashews.

Place lemon juice in a small bowl with olive oil, cinnamon, allspice, salt, and pepper mix until well combined then add to salad.

---

**Fun Fact:**

In Greek myths Menthe, a water Nymph who resided in the river of the underworld, had an affair with Hades. When Persephone, Hades' wife, found out she turned Menthe into the mint plant by stepping down on her with all her might.

# Wild Rice Salad with Cauliflower & Walnuts

*Preparation: 20 Min.*  *Makes 4-6 Servings*

## Ingredients

- ½ c. sprouted wild rice
- ½ c. cauliflower
- ½ c. parsley
- ½ c. pitted raw olives
- ¼ c. cold pressed olive oil
- ¼ c. walnuts, chopped
- ½ c. tomato
- ½ lemon, juiced
- ½ tsp. cumin
- Himalayan crystal salt to taste
- pepper to taste
- ¼ tsp. tarragon
- ¼ tsp. rosemary
- ¼ c. nut mayo

## Directions

Sprout black wild rice. Rinse off rice and place in large bowl.

Toss coarsely chop cauliflower, parsley, olives, and tomato with rice.

Season with salt, pepper, cumin, lemon, and olive oil. Transfer to a serving bowl garnish with whole parsley leaves.

# Sprouted Kamut Salad with Vinaigrette

Preparation: 20 Min.  Makes 8-12 Servings

## Ingredients

### Salad

- 1 c. kamut or wheat berries, sprouted 2-4 days
- ¾ c. red bell pepper
- ¾ c. yellow bell pepper
- ¾ c. small summer squash
- ¾ c. tomatoes

### Vinaigrette

- 3 tbsp. cold pressed olive oil
- 3 tbsp. raw apple cider vinegar
- 2 tbsp. onion powder
- 1 tbsp. pure water
- 1 tbsp. mustard powder
- 1 tbsp. garlic powder
- 1 tsp. cayenne pepper
- 1 tsp. thyme
- ½ tsp. Himalayan crystal salt
- black pepper to taste

## Directions

Sprout Kamut (wheat) for about 2 days or until soft.

In a small bowl, mix vinegar, olive oil, onion powder, water, mustard powder, garlic powder, cayenne pepper, thyme, salt, and pepper with a fork or spoon until well mixed.

Cut red and yellow bell peppers into strips, slice squash and chop tomatoes then place in a bowl. Add sprouted Kamut and toss together. Pour vinaigrette over salad and chill at least 3 hours.

---

*Fun Fact:*

Kamut was originally cultivated in the Fertile Crescent area which runs from Egypt to the Tigris-Euphrates valley. Kamut is actually a modern-day brand name.

---

# Quinoa Salad

*Preparation:* Makes 4-6
10 Min.  Servings

## Ingredients

- ½ c. quinoa, sprouted or cooked
- 1 c. chickpeas, spouted
- 1 c. English cucumber, diced
- 1 c. pomegranate seeds
- 1 avocado, diced
- ½ c. fresh parsley, chopped
- ½ c. fresh mint, chopped
- 2 tsp. cold pressed olive oil
- 1 lemon, juiced
- ½ tsp. raw apple cider vinegar
- 1 tsp. Himalayan crystal salt
- 1 tsp. pepper

## Directions

Sprout quinoa and chickpeas drain water off and put in a bowl.

In a large bowl, combine quinoa, chickpeas, avocado, cucumber, pomegranate seeds, parsley, and mint.

In a small bowl, whisk olive oil, lemon, and vinegar together. Drizzle over salad.

Serve with salt and pepper. Serve chilled or room temperature. Store leftovers in refrigerator for 2-3 days

# Flora's Albanian Salad

Preparation: Makes 2-4
10 Min.     Servings

## Ingredients

- 3 cucumbers, sliced
- 1 yellow squash, thinly sliced
- 2 tomatoes, sliced
- ½ red bell pepper
- ½ orange, or yellow bell pepper
- 4 tbsp. cold pressed olive oil
- 3 tbsp. raw apple cider vinegar
- Himalayan crystal salt to taste
- black pepper to taste

## Directions

Slice cucumbers, yellow squash, tomatoes, red, orange, and yellow bell pepper then place into a bowl.

In a small jar with a lid, place oil, vinegar, salt, and pepper. Put lid on jar and shake until well mixed. Pour dressing over vegetables and toss. Arrange on a plate and serve.

# Orange Cucumber Salad

Preparation: 20 Min.    Makes 8-12 Servings

## Ingredients

- 1 c. cucumber, thinly sliced
- ¼ tsp. Himalayan crystal salt
- dash black pepper
- 2 medium oranges, peeled and sectioned
- ½ red bell pepper, chopped
- 2 tbsp. parsley
- ¼ tsp. thyme
- 1 head lettuce
- ½ c nut mayo (page 112)

## Directions

Sprinkle cucumber with salt and pepper, toss in orange sections, red pepper, parsley, thyme, black pepper, and nut mayo then mix. Serve on lettuce.

# Apple Zucchini Salad

*Preparation:*    *Makes 6-8*
*15 Min.*      *Servings*

## Ingredients

### Dressing

- 1 tbsp. cold pressed olive oil
- 1 tbsp. lemon, juiced
- 1 lime, juiced
- 1 tsp. nutmeg
- 1 tsp. basil
- ¼ tsp. pepper

### Salad

- 3 medium apples, cored and diced
- ½ medium red onion, chopped
- 1 red bell pepper, chopped
- 1 pound zucchini, sliced thinly

## Directions

To make the dressing, juice lime and lemon and place juice in a large salad bowl. Then add oil, nutmeg, basil, and pepper mix well.

Cut and core apples and place in the same bowl with dressing and coat them well.

Cut and prepare onion, bell pepper and zucchini then place in the bowl with apples and dressing and gently toss. Serve and in enjoy.

# Kale Strawberry Salad

*Preparation: Makes 4-6*
*10 Min.      Servings*

## Ingredients

- 2-3 c. strawberries, halved
- 1 bunch kale
- 1 c. pecans
- ¼ c. basil
- 1 tsp. cold pressed olive oil
- strawberry dressing (page 97, optional)

## Directions

Wash kale and remove thick stem. Massage, or rub, in olive oil into each leaf. Tear kale into bite sized pieces and place them in the bowl.

Slice strawberries and chop basil. Toss kale, strawberries, and basil together.

Place salad on a plate and top with pecans that have been soaked and dried. May dress with strawberry dressing.

---

### Fun Fact

The history of the strawberry dates back to Ancient Rome where the fruit was considered the symbol of Venus, the goddess of love, because of its bright red color and enticing taste.

Later, the berry became a symbol of fertility due to its many exterior seeds.

Legend has it that if you break a double strawberry in half and share it with a member of the opposite sex, you will fall in love with each other.

Strawberries are still considered an aphrodisiac today. There was once a tradition in the French countryside, of serving newlyweds cold strawberry soup to help honeymoon romance.

# Zoodle Salad

Preparation: 15 Min.  Makes 4-6 Servings

## Ingredients

### Sauce

- ¼ c. dried tomatoes
- 1 tbsp. cold pressed olive oil
- ¼ c. avocado
- 3 tbsp. lemon, juiced

### Salad

- 3 c. tomatoes, chopped
- 2 cucumbers, sliced
- 2 small zucchinis, shredded

## Directions

Soak dried tomatoes in enough pure water to cover for about 10 minutes. Remove tomatoes and place in a blender. Reserve soaking water from tomatoes for later use.

To tomatoes add olive oil, avocado, and lemon juice and mix until well blended. Add tomato soaking water until a creamy textured is achieved.

Chop fresh tomatoes, slice cumberers and zoodle zucchini, and then, place in a bowl. Pour sauce over salad and mix.

# Three-Pepper Zoddle Salad

*Preparation:* *Makes 4-6*
*20 Min.* *Servings*

## Ingredients

- 2 c. zucchini, zoodled
- 1 tbsp. cold pressed olive oil
- 1 red bell pepper, cut into ¼ inch strips
- 1 orange bell pepper, cut into ¼ inch strips
- 1 yellow bell pepper, cut into ¼ inch strips
- ¼ c. dried tomatoes
- ½ c. fresh tomatoes
- ¼ tsp. oregano
- ½ tsp. basil
- ¼ tsp. Himalayan crystal salt
- 1 tbsp. onion, chopped
- garnish with basil leave and ramasan (page 118)

## Directions

Soak dried tomatoes in water for 30 minutes. Remove tomatoes from water but save the soaking water for later use.

Place soaked tomatoes in a blender with fresh tomatoes, onion, basil, oregano, and salt mix until smooth, adding tomato soaking water if need to achieve smooth texture.

Cut bell peppers into ¼ inch strips and place in a bowl. Pour blender mixture over bell peppers and gently mix.

Using a spiral slicer and make zoodles, this makes the zucchini look like spaghetti. May shred zucchini if desired.

Place zoodles on plate and top with bell pepper mixture. Top with fresh basil and rawmasan.

---

**Fun Fact:**

Bell peppers are part of the night shade family. Red/yellow/orange bell peppers are simply green bell peppers that have been left on the vine to ripen.

---

# Tomato Stuffed with Cabbage Salad

**Preparation:** 15 Min.    Makes 2-4 Servings

## Ingredients

- 2-4 ripe tomatoes
- 1 clove garlic
- 3 c. savoy cabbage
- 1 green onion
- ½ tsp. Himalayan crystal salt
- black pepper to taste
- ¼ c. nut mayo (page 112)

## Directions

Wash and cut tomatoes, leaving the bottom connected and set aside. It should kind of look like a flower.

Wash and shred cabbage using a mandolin, place in a bowl.

Mince garlic and thinly slice green onion add to cabbage. Add salt and pepper. Gently mix in nut mayo.

Place cabbage salad in the middle of the cut tomato and serve.

# Herbed Tomato Salad

Preparation: 10 Min.  Makes 2-4 Servings

## Ingredients

- 4 large tomatoes, sliced
- 1 small red onion, thinly sliced
- 4 tbsp. fresh basil, chopped
- 2 tbsp. fresh tarragon, chopped
- 4 tbsp. cold pressed olive oil
- 2 tbsp. raw apple cider vinegar
- Himalayan crystal salt to taste
- black pepper to taste

## Directions

Thinly slice onion and separate the rings. Arrange tomatoes slice on plate. Place onion rings over tomatoes. Sprinkle with basil and tarragon.

In a jar with a lid, mix raw apple cider vinegar, cold pressed olive oil, salt, and pepper. Place the lid on the jar and shake it up. Pour dressing over the salad.

# Adam's Pomegranate Salad

Preparation: 20 Min.  Makes 4-6 Servings

## Ingredients

- 1 apple, cut into wedges
- ¼ to ½ pomegranate, seeded
- ¼ c. red currents or raspberries

## Directions

Arrange apple slices on a plate, in a circle fan. Sprinkle pomegranate seeds over that and lastly place raspberries in the center of the dish.

---

Fun Fact:

The word pomegranate means apple with many seeds.

---

# Mediterranean Vegetable Salad

Preparation: 20 Min.  Makes 2-4 Servings

## Ingredients

- ¼ c. raw apple cider vinegar
- 1 tbsp. cold pressed olive oil
- 2 tbsp. oregano leaves, fresh and chopped
- ¼ tsp. mustard seed, ground
- ½ tsp. Himalayan crystal salt
- ½ tsp. black pepper
- 1 clove garlic
- 1 orange bell pepper, sliced into thin rings
- 1 yellow bell peppers, sliced into thin rings
- 2 large tomatoes, sliced
- ½ c. butter lettuce
- ¼ c. vegan feta cheese (page 116)
- ¼ c. sundried olives

## Directions

Make feta cheese and set aside.

In jar with a lid place raw apple cider vinegar, olive oil, oregano, mustard, salt, and pepper put lid on jar and mix well.

In a bowl, place bell pepper rings and pour dressing over and toss. Cover and refrigerate at least an hour.

Line plates with butter lettuce and sliced tomatoes. Remove bell peppers from dressing and place the peppers over the lettuce.

Sprinkle with vegan feta cheese and olives.

---

**Fun Fact:**

Legend has it, the Greek goddess Aphrodite created aromatic oregano as a symbol of joy and grew it in her garden on Mount Olympus. One of the ancient Greek names for oregano was panakes or "all heal".

---

# Brussels Sprout Hazelnut Salad

Preparation: Makes 4-6
15 Min.  Servings

## Ingredients

- 1 c. Brussels sprouts
- ½ c. hazelnuts
- 1 tbsp. olive oil
- 1 tsp. coconut nectar
- 1 ½ tsp. thyme
- ½ tsp. Himalayan crystal salt
- ¼ tsp. black pepper
- 2 tbsp. basil
- 2 tsp. turmeric

## Directions

Cut hazelnuts in half and soak overnight. Drain water off hazelnuts.

Wash and tear leaves off Brussels sprouts and place in a bowl.

To Brussels sprouts add hazelnuts, olive oil, lemon juice, coconut nectar, thyme, salt, pepper, basil, and turmeric toss until everything is well coated and let marinate for at least an hour.

# Taco Salad

Preparation: Makes 2-4
20 Min.    Servings

## Ingredients

- 1 head lettuce, torn into bite sized pieces.
- 2 avocados, sliced
- 4 tomatoes, sliced
- salsa (page 110)
- sour cream (page 113)
- sunflower beans (page 111)
- sundried olives (optional)

## Directions

Make sunflower beans and set aside. Wash lettuce, tear into bite sized pieces and place on a plate.

Place a scoopful of sunflower beans onto center of plate on top of lettuce. Make salsa and place on top of beans.

Arrange tomato, avocado slices, and olive round beans. Drizzle sour cream over the top.

---

**Fun Fact:**

Olives only become truly edible after curing. The raw fruit has oleuropein, a bitter compound that must be removed prior to eating.

There are various methods of curing, including oil-cured, water-cured, brine-cured, dry-cured (salt), and lye-cured,

Green olives, which are young, immature olives, can be cured in water, which removes the bitter taste of the raw fruit. Brine curing is used with green olives as well as ripe (purple or black) olives.

The longer the olive is permitted to ferment in its own brine, the less bitter and more intricate its flavor will become.

---

# Apple Walnut Salad

Preparation: 20 Min.    Makes 4-6 Servings

## Ingredients

- 1 head lettuce, torn into bite sized pieces
- 3 medium apples, sliced thinly
- ¼ c. walnuts, soaked then dried
- ¼ c. fresh apple Juice
- Himalayan crystal salt to taste
- pepper to taste

## Directions

In a bowl, mix lettuce, apple, nuts, salt, and pepper. Pour the apple juice over the salad and toss.

---

# Kale Salad

Preparation: 20 Min.    Makes 2-4 Servings

## Ingredients

- 1 Mandarin orange, peeled and segmented
- 1 small carrot, shredded
- 4 c. kale
- ½ tsp. Himalayan crystal salt
- 1 tsp. cold pressed olive oil
- ¼ tsp. pepper
- pecans

## Directions

Wash kale and remove the thick stem. Massage, or rub in the olive oil into each leaf. Tear up kale into bite-sized pieces and place them in the bowl. Toss kale, carrot, salt, and pepper together.

Place the salad on a plate and top with pecans that have been soaked and dried along with orange segments.

# Wild Rice & Brussel Sprout Salad

Preparation: 20 Min.    Makes 4-6 Servings

## Ingredients

- 1 ¼ c. wild rice, sprouted
- 2 tbsp. raw apple cider vinegar
- ½ c. red onion
- 2 c. Brussels sprouts
- 8 radishes
- 1 lemon
- ¼ c. mint
- ¼ c. parsley
- ¼ c. basil
- ¼ c. sunflower sprouts
- ¼ c. pea sprouts
- ½ c. dried cranberries
- 2 tsp. cold pressed olive oil
- pinch of Himalayan crystal salt

## Directions

Soak and sprout wild rice, drain water off the rice and set aside. Finely slice red onion using a mandolin and place in a bowl, add vinegar, then mix together set aside.

Shred Brussels sprouts and radishes using mandolin and place in the bowl with onion. Add lemon juice and salt then stir to mix. Chop mint, parsley, and basil and add to the Brussels sprouts. Add sprouted rice to the bowl. Toss sunflower and pea sprouts along with dry cranberries into the rice and herbs. Drizzle olive oil then stir and serve.

# Smart Cat Salad

Preparation:   Makes 4-6
25 Min.        Servings

## Ingredients

- 1 c. garbanzo beans
- 1 c. cucumber
- ¼ c. red onion
- 1 c. cherry tomatoes
- ½ c. broccoli
- 3 c. lettuce
- ½ c. cauliflower
- ½ c. radish
- 1 bell pepper, red or range
- sprouts
- creamy lemon poppy seed dressing (page 99)

## Directions

Sprout garbanzo beans, they should be soft and easily smashed with a fork.

Wash lettuce and place in a bowl or on a plate. Slice cucumber, onion, radish, and bell pepper arrange on top of the lettuce. Cut cauliflower and broccoli into small pieces and sprinkle over the salad along with cherry tomatoes and garbanzo beans.

Make lemon poppy seed dressing and pour over the top of the salad.

## Note

### Sprouting garbanzo beans

Soak garbanzo beans overnight. Drain and rinse them thoroughly.

Invert jar over a bowl at an angle so that the beans will drain and still allow air to circulate.

Repeat rinsing and draining 2-3 times per day until sprouts are the desired length, usually 3-6 days.

# Z Spinach Salad

## Ingredients

### Salad

- 3 c. mixed baby lettuce and spinach
- 1 c. zucchini, cubed
- ½ c. strawberries, halved
- ½ c. walnuts, soaked and then dried
- ¼ c. small red onion, thinly sliced

### Strawberry Dressing

- ½ c. fresh strawberries
- 1 tbsp. lime juice
- 2 tbsp. coconut nectar
- ½ c. zucchini
- 1 tsp. poppy seeds
- Himalayan crystal salt to taste
- white pepper to taste

## Directions

Combine ½ cup strawberries, lime juice, coconut nectar, zucchini, poppy seeds, salt and pepper in a blender and mix well.

While blender is running, slowly add water until desired texture is achieved.

Wash baby lettuces and spinach, cut zucchini, ½ cup strawberries, and onion then place in a bowl with walnuts.

Add dressing to salad just before serving.

---

**Fun Fact:**

Archaeological evidence of zucchini is found as far back and 7,000 years ago in South America.

---

# Island Green Salad

## Ingredients

### Salad

- 4 c. mixed salad greens
- 1 ½ c. Mandarin orange slices

### Island Dressing

- ½ c. cold pressed olive oil
- 2 limes, juiced
- 1 tbsp. ginger, grated
- 3 cloves garlic, minced
- ¼ c. raw liquid sweetener (optional)

## Directions

In a jar with a lid combine oil, lime juice, ginger, garlic, and raw sweetener place lid on the jar and shake well. Chill dressing until serving time.

Peel and segment oranges then set aside. Wash green and place them in a large bowl. Add orange segments to the greens.

Shake the dressing well before pouring over salad. Pour dressing over the top of the greens just before serving.

---

*Fun Fact:*

*Mandarin oranges—in all their forms, and there are many, are probably descended from wild oranges that grew in northeast India as long as 3,000 years ago.*

# Greek Salad

Preparation: 25 Min.   Makes 4-6 Servings

## Ingredients

### Salad

- 1 head crisp lettuce, torn into bite sized pieces
- 1 red bell pepper, sliced
- 4 tomatoes cut into wedges
- 1 red onion, sliced into rings
- sundried olives (optional)
- ½ c. vegan basil feta cheese (page 116, optional)

### Greek Dressing

- ½ c raw tahini
- 1 lemon, juiced
- ½ tsp. ground cumin
- ½ tsp. paprika
- 1 clove garlic
- 4 tbsp. cold pressed olive oil
- ½ c. pure water
- pinch Himalayan crystal salt

## Directions

Make vegan basil feta cheese and set aside.

Slice bell pepper, red onion, and chop tomatoes place in a large bowl. Toss lettuce with bell peppers.

In a blender, place tahini, olive oil, lemon juice, cumin, paprika, garlic, salt, and water blend until creamy. Pour dressing over the salad.

Crumble feta and sliced olives over the top.

---

**Fun Fact:**

The ancient Greeks and Romans thought that eating lettuce helped you to have a good night's sleep.

---

# Fiesta Salad

Preparation: 30 Min.    Makes 4-6 Servings

## Ingredients

### Salad

- 1 ½ c. spring mix
- 1 ½ c. favorite lettuce
- 1 avocado, cubed
- 1 c. cherry tomatoes
- ½ c. sundried olives, sliced
- lime slices, garnish
- 5 artichoke hearts, chopped (frozen or water packed optional not a raw product)
- ½ c. vegan basil feta cheese (page 116, optional)

### Fiesta Dressing

- 2 tbsp. cold pressed olive oil
- 1 green onion, chopped
- 1 lime, juiced
- Himalayan crystal salt to taste
- white pepper to taste
- ½ tsp. cumin, ground
- ½tsp. chili powder
- ½1 tbsp. cilantro, finely chopped

## Directions

In a small bowl, mix olive oil, green onion, lime juice, cilantro, cumin, chili powder, salt, and pepper.

In a large bowl, combine spring mix, lettuce, tomatoes, olives, and artichokes.

Pour Fiesta Dressing over salad and let mingle about 30 minutes. Add avocado and feta just before serving. Garnish with lime slices.

# Vegetable Ribbon Salad

*Preparation:* *Makes 2-4*
*10 Min.* *Servings*

## Ingredients

**Salad**

- 1 c. carrots, thinly sliced
- 1 c. zucchini, zooodles
- ½ c. beet, zoodled
- 2 c. cabbage, thinly sliced
- 1 avocado, thinly sliced

**Dressing**

- 1 clove garlic
- ¼ c. basil, fresh
- 4 tbsp. parsley
- ½ lemon, juiced
- Salt and pepper to taste

## Directions

Use a spiralizer to make thin strips of zucchini and beets. Thinly slice carrots with a knife, vegetable peeler or mandolin lengthwise.

Shred cabbage using a mandolin or knife. Place in a bowl then add zucchini, carrots, and beets. Toss with dressing just before serving.

Thinly slice avocado and layer over top of the salad.

In a blender, combine garlic, basil, leek, parsley, salt, pepper, and lemon juice until well mixed. Pour dressing over salad.

# Beet Salad with Dill Dressing

Preparation: 20 Min.    Marinating: 30 Min    Makes 4-6 Servings

## Ingredients

### Salad

- 3 beets, mixed colors if possible, thinly sliced
- clove garlic, minced
- 4 c. arugula leaves
- 2 tbsp. cold pressed olive oil
- 1 avocado, peeled and sliced
- ¼ tsp. Himalayan crystal salt

### Dill Dressing

- ½ c. nut mayo (page 112)
- 1 clove garlic, minced
- 1 tbsp. fresh dill, chopped
- Himalayan crystal salt to taste
- black pepper to taste
- 1 lemon, juiced

## Directions

Marinate thinly sliced beets in cold pressed olive oil, lemon juice, salt and minced garlic for 30 minutes.

Combine mayo, garlic, dill, salt, pepper, and lemon juice in a small bowl and set aside.

Arrange greens on a platter, and then place beets and avocado slices on top. Drizzle dill dressing over the top and serve.

---

**Fun Facts:**

Beetroot contains betaine, a substance that relaxes the mind and is used in other forms to treat depression. It also contains tryptophan, which is also found in chocolate and contributes to a sense of well-being.

---

# Layered Salad

Preparation: Makes 4-6
20 Min.      Servings

## Ingredients

### Salad

- 4 c. butter lettuce, torn
- 2 c. peas, fresh or frozen
- ½ c. raw pumpkin seeds
- ½ c. radishes, sliced
- 1 ½ c. cauliflower flowerets
- 1 c. broccoli flowerets
- ½ c. carrots, shredded
- cherry tomatoes, garnish

### Dressing

- ½ c. nut mayo (page 112)
- 1 clove garlic
- 3 tbsp. raw pumpkin seeds
- ¾ c. peas, fresh or frozen
- ½ lemon, juiced
- ½ tsp. Himalayan crystal salt

## Directions

Place butter lettuce on the bottom of a clear bowl. Layer peas, pumpkin seed, sliced radishes, cauliflower florets, broccoli florets and carrots.

In a blender, combine nut mayo, garlic, 3 tbsp. pumpkin seeds, peas, lemon juice, and salt blend until smooth adding water if needed.

Place the dressing on top of layered salad and garnish with cherry tomatoes. Toss just before serving.

---

*Fun Fact:*

Cauliflower comes in 4 different colors the white most people know. Orange that contains the most beta carotene out of all the variants. Purple are filled with anthocyanins, an antioxidant. Green has the appearance of cauliflower but the chlorophyll content of broccoli.

# Root Salad with Arugula

Preparation:    Drying:    Makes 4-6
30 Min.      2-4 Hrs.    Servings

## Ingredients

- 4-6 c. baby arugula
- 4 cloves garlic, crushed
- ½ pound parsnips, cut into bite sized pieces
- 2 medium beets, cut into bite sized pieces
- 2 medium turnips, cut into bite sized pieces
- 1 small rutabaga, peeled and cut into bite sized pieces
- 1 tbsp. rosemary
- 4 tbsp. basil
- 1 tsp. black pepper
- 2 tbsp. lemon, juiced
- 3-5 tbsp. cold pressed olive oil

## Directions

Place parsnips, beets, turnips, and rutabaga, in a baking dish. Sprinkle with 3 Tbsp. of the oil, rosemary, garlic, and pepper. Dehydrate for about 5 hours.

In a large bowl, combine arugula, basil, lemon juice and the reaming 2 tbsp. of oil toss and place on serving plate. Top with dried vegetables.

## Variation

Spinach or kale may be used in place of arugula.

---

**Fun Fact:**

The health benefits of arugula include diabetes management, osteoporosis prevention, cardiovascular health, prevention of cancer, improve vision, boost the immune system, improve digestion, aid weight loss, good for bone health, helps reduce inflammation in the body and protects the aging brain from cognitive decline.

---

# Zucchini and Carrot Salad

*Preparation:*   *Makes 2-4*
*20 Min.*     *Servings*

## Ingredients

- 2 medium carrots, cut into julienne strips
- 4 medium zucchinis, cut into julienne strips
- 1 tbsp. parsley, fresh or dried
- 1 tsp. dill weed, fresh or dried
- 1 tsp. basil, fresh or dried
- 1 lemon, juiced
- ¼ tsp. Himalayan crystal salt
- ¼ tsp. black pepper
- ¼ tsp. turmeric
- 1 tbsp. cold pressed olive oil

## Directions

Thinly slice carrots and cut zucchini into strips and place in a bowl.

Finely chop fresh basil, dill, parsley, and place in a jar with a lid. To the jar add lemon juice, salt, turmeric, and olive oil place lid on jar and shake well.

Pour dressing over the carrots and zucchini.

# Early Summer Salad

Preparation: Makes 4-6
20 Min.     Servings

## Ingredients

### Salad

- 1 red bell pepper, sliced
- ¼ c. radishes, sliced
- 1 cucumber, sliced
- 1 c. lettuce
- ¼ c. olives
- ¼ c. microgreen sprouts

### Honey Dressing

- ¾ c. cashews
- 1 tbsp. mustard powder
- 1 tbsp. lemon juice
- ¼ tsp. Himalayan crystal salt
- 1 tbsp. raw honey or another raw liquid sweetener
- ½ c. water

## Directions

Prepare vegetables by washing and slicing bell pepper, radishes, olives, and cucumbers.

Place lettuce on bottom of the plate. Arrange vegetables in rows over lettuce. Top with sprouts.

To make honey dressing place cashews, mustard powder, lemon juice, salt, and honey in a blender and slowly add water until desired texture is achieved.

Fun Facts:

Ancient Egyptian records show that radishes were a common food in Egypt before the pyramids were built. Partly because of a mistaken belief that the heat in radishes' taste made them an especially high energy food.

# Cucumber Salad

*Preparation: 20 Min.*   *Makes 2-4 Servings*

## Ingredients

- 1 c. almond sour cream (page 113)
- ½ lemon, juice
- 1 tsp. dill weed, fresh
- Himalayan crystal salt to taste
- 3 c. cucumbers, thinly sliced
- ¼ c. red onion, thinly sliced

## Directions

In a large bowl, place sour cream, lemon juice, dill, and salt stir with a spoon to combine.

Thinly slice cucumbers and red onion then place in bowl with sour cream and gently mix until well coated.

# Old Fashioned "Potato" Salad

Preparation: 20 Min.   Makes 6-8 Servings

## Ingredients

- 1 large jicama, peeled and cubed
- 3 stocks celery, sliced
- 2 green onions, chopped
- 2 medium cucumbers, sliced
- 1 small red, yellow, or orange bell pepper
- 6 radishes
- ½ tsp. raw apple cider vinegar
- 1 ½ tsp. mustard powder
- 1 tbsp. dill
- 1 ½ c. nut mayo (page 112)
- Himalayan crystal salt to taste
- black pepper to taste

## Directions

Make nut mayo and place in a bowl. Add dill, mustard powder, vinegar, salt, and pepper and mix.

Peel and cube jicama, make sure cubes are small and bite sized. Place jicama in a bowl and mix with nut mayo.

Thinly slice celery, cucumbers, bell pepper, radishes, and chop green onions. Mix with jicama then refrigerate and serve.

## Note

Choose jicama that is firm has few spots and no kicks or broken skin. A nice smooth tan color is desirable. As jicama ages it will wrinkle, dry out and spots will darken.

# Eggless Salad

*Preparation:*    *Soaking:*    *Makes 8-12*
*15 Min.*    *8-12 Hrs.*    *Servings*

## Ingredients

- 2 c. sesame seed pulp, from making milk
- 1 red bell pepper, chopped
- 1 small celery, sliced
- 2 green onions, chopped
- 1 tbsp. parsley
- 1 tbsp. dill
- 1 tsp. mustard seed powder
- 1 tbsp. turmeric
- 2 tsp. lovage
- ¼ c. nut mayo (page 112)

## Directions

Place sesame seed pulp saved from making sesame milk in a bowl. Chop bell peppers, green onions, parsley, and shredded carrots place in a bowl with sesame pulp.

Add dill, mustard seed powder, turmeric, lovage, and nut mayo mix well. Adjust seasonings to taste. Enjoy as a refreshing salad or stuff it in a tomato or bell pepper.

## Note

The herb lovage is the real secret to this sesame salad tasting like eggs.

# Broccoli Salad

Preparation: Makes 4-6
20 Min. Servings

## Ingredients

- 10 slices Nadhirrah's eggplant baykon (page 109)
- 1 head fresh broccoli, cut into bite size pieces
- ¼ c. red onion, chopped
- 1 c. nut mayo (page 112)
- 1 c. sunflower seeds, soaked then dried

## Directions

Prepare Nadhirrah's baykon then crumble and set aside. In a medium bowl, combine broccoli, and onion.

In a small bowl, whisk together vinegar and mayo. Pour over broccoli mixture, and toss until well mixed.

Refrigerate for at least two hours. Before serving, toss salad with crumbled bacon and sunflower seeds.

# Carrot Raisin Salad

Preparation: Makes 4-6
15 Min. Servings

## Ingredients

- 1 c. raisins
- 2 apples, shredded
- 3 large carrots, shredded
- ½ c. nut mayo (page 112)
- Himalayan crystal salt

## Directions

Shred carrots and apples and place in a medium bowl, add raisins.

Gently mix nut mayo and salt. Chill a few hours before serving.

## Note

If raisins are hard, soak for 10 minutes to soften then drain off water.

# "Tuna" Salad

*Preparation:*   *Soaking*   *Makes 2-4*
*15 Min.*    *8-12 Hrs.*   *Servings*

## Ingredients

**"Tuna"**

- 1 c. sunflower seeds soaked overnight
- ¼ c. onion, minced
- Himalayan crystal salt to taste
- 1 lemon, juiced
- 2 stocks of celery
- 1 tbsp. kelp
- 1 zucchini

**Salad**

- 2 c. lettuce
- ½ c. radishes
- ¼ c. celery
- 1 avocado, sliced
- 2 tomatoes, sliced

## Directions

Soak sunflower seeds overnight. Drain water and rinse. Place the seeds in food processor.

Cut celery into half inch pieces. Add celery, onion, salt, lemon juice, zucchini, and kelp to food processor and blend. It should be roughly mixed.

Wash and tear lettuce into bite-sized pieces and palace on a plate. Scoop about ½ cup of the tuna onto the center of the plate. Place radishes and tomatoes around. May use sliced avocado if you wish. Place a few slices of celery on the top of the tuna.

## Variations

1) Instead of using sunflower seeds try walnuts or mix of both then mix as directed. If no zucchini is available may use ¾ c. nut mayo in place.

2) To make a **tuna wrap**, take the romaine leaf lettuce and place the tuna mixture down the spine. On top of that add sliced tomato and avocado. Roll the lettuce leaf and enjoy.

# Waldorf Salad

Preparation: Makes 4-6
30 Min.    Servings

## Ingredients

- ½ c. nut mayo
- ½ lemon, juiced
- 2 c. apples, coarsely chopped
- 1 c. celery, chopped
- 1 c. grapes
- ½ c. pecans or walnuts, soaked, dried and chopped

## Directions

In a bowl, combine apples, lemon, celery, and grapes. Mix in nut mayo until everything covered.

Chop pecans or walnuts and sprinkle over the top.

## Variation

1) Chop up and add 1-cup pineapple, 1 pear, 2 kiwi fruits for a festive fruity waldrof salad.

2) You can use orange juice in place of the nut mayo if desired.

---

# Strawberry Kiwi Salad

Preparation: Makes
5 Min.    2-4Servings

## Ingredients

- 1 banana
- ¾ c. strawberries
- 2 kiwi
- ¼ c. dried coconut (optional)

## Directions

Peel and slice kiwi and banana placing in a bowl. Wash and slice strawberries and add to kiwi and banana. Sprinkle with coconut if desired.

# Fruit Salad with Peach Dressing

*Preparation:  Makes 4-6*
*20 Min.      Servings*

## Ingredients

### Salad

- 1 c. strawberries, halved
- 1 c. peach slices
- 1 c. grapes
- 4 oranges, sliced
- 5 c. mixed greens (optional)

### Peach Dressing

- ½ c. cashew cream (page 111)
- ¼ c. peach pulp (saved from juicing)
- 3 tbsp. water or peach juice
- 2 tsp. raw liquid sweetener
- ¼ c. nut mayo

## Directions

Make cashew cream and place in a small bowl. Gently combine peach pulp, peach juice, and sweetener set aside.

Slice strawberries and peaches. Peel and segment oranges and place in a large bowl. Add grapes and mix in the dressing and set aside.

This can be served with just the fruit or on top of spring greens. Divide greens and place on plate and top with fruit.

# Ambrosia Salad

Preparation:  Makes 4-6
20 Min.    Servings

## Ingredients

- 2 oranges, peeled and sectioned
- 1 c. unsweetened coconut, shredded
- 2 c. cashew cream (page 111)

## Directions

Make cashew cream and set aside.

Peel and section oranges and place in a bowl. Gently combine cashew cream and then add coconut.

## Variation

For **pineapple ambrosia**

- substitute 1 pineapple cut into chunks for the oranges.

For **lemon ambrosia** add

- 2 lemons, peeled and sectioned
- ½ c. golden raisins
- 4 tbsp. raw coconut nectar
- omit the oranges

For **pomegranate ambrosia** add

- 1 c.  pomegranate seeds
- 4 tbsp. raw coconut nectar
- omit the oranges

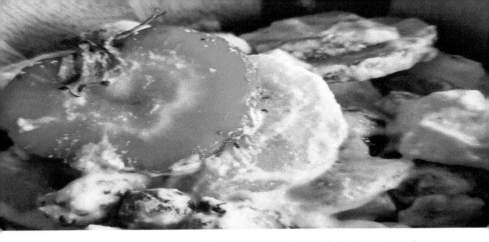

# Creamy Fruit Salad with Vanilla Dressing

Preparation: 20 Min.　Makes 4-6 Servings

## Ingredients

- 1 c. strawberries, quartered
- 1 c. blueberries
- 1 c. blackberries
- 1 c. mandarin orange, peeled and segmented
- 2 kiwis, peeled and sliced
- 2 c. pineapple, chunked
- 1 c. red grapes
- 1 c. almonds, peeled and soaked
- 1 vanilla bean or 1 tbsp. pure vanilla extract
- 1 tbsp. coconut nectar
- ½ -1 c. water

## Directions

Soak almonds overnight in water, drain water off. While brown skin is still wet peel it off.

Place peeled almonds in a blender along with vanilla, coconut nectar, and water. Combine until very creamy.

In a large bowl, combine strawberries, blueberries, blackberries, oranges, kiwi, pineapple, and grapes. Pour blender mixture over the salad and gently mix.

## Note

If making ahead of time mix in dressing no more than 4 hours before serving.

# Hot and Spicy Dressing

Preparation: 10 Min.   Makes 1-2 Cups

## Ingredients

- 1 c. nut mayo (page 112)
- ¼ c. pure water
- 1 ½ tbsp. raw apple cider vinegar
- ¾ hot pepper
- ¼ c. onion
- 1 clove garlic
- 1 red, orange, or yellow bell pepper
- 2 stocks celery

## Directions

In a blender, combine mayo, water, vinegar, hot pepper, onion, garlic, bell pepper, and celery then until smooth.

# Green Goddess Dressing

Preparation: 10 Min.   Makes 1-2 Cups

## Ingredients

- 2 green onions
- ½ jalapeno pepper
- ½ c. almond sour cream (page 113)
- ¼ c. cilantro
- 1 avocado
- 2 limes, juiced
- ½ tsp. Himalayan crystal salt

## Directions

In a blender, combine green onion, jalapeno, sour cream, cilantro, lime juice, salt, and peeled and pitted avocado until well mixed. Add water if needed to thin.

# Herbed Hazelnut Dressing

Preparation: 10 Min.  Soaking: 8-12 Hrs.  Makes 1-2 Cups

## Ingredients

- 3 tbsp. cold pressed olive oil
- ½ c. hazelnuts, soaked
- 1 lemon, juiced
- 1 tbsp. parsley
- 1 ½ tbsp. basil
- ½ tbsp. fresh dill
- ½ tsp. Himalayan crystal salt
- 2 green onion
- 1 clove garlic
- ½ c. pure water

## Directions

Soak hazelnuts overnight then drain off the water. Place nuts, oil, water, garlic, and salt in a blender.

Juice the lemon and add to the blender combine until well-mixed adding water if needed to achieve the thickness desired. Add green onion, dill, basil, and parsley to the blender then pulse to combine.

## Note

Use fresh herbs if available. If winter use dried herbs.

# Green Dressing

Preparation: 10 Min.  Makes 1-2 Cups

## Ingredients

- 1 c. mayo
- 1 large avocado
- 1 c. spinach
- 1 lime, juiced
- 1 small cucumber
- enough pure water to blend

## Directions

In a blender, combine mayo, spinach, lime juice, avocado, and cucumber blend until smooth.

# Lavender Dressing

Preparation: Makes 1-2
10 Min.        Cups

## Ingredients

- 2 c. cashews
- ½ c. cold pressed olive oil
- 1 tsp. Himalayan crystal salt
- 1 tsp. onion powder
- ¼ tsp lavender flowers soaked
- 1 tsp. raw apple cider vinegar
- 1 clove garlic
- 1 lemon, juiced

## Directions

Soak lavender flowers in ½ cup olive oil for 30 minutes.

In a blender, combine salt, onion powder, raw apple cider vinegar, garlic, and lemon juice until smooth.

Add lavender flowers and olive oil and continue blending and tell desired smoothness is achieved.

---

# Tahini

Preparation: Makes 1-2
10 Min.        Cups

## Ingredients

- ¾ c. sesame seeds
- 2 tbsp. cold pressed olive oil
- 1 tsp. Himalayan crystal salt
- 1 lemon, juiced
- ¼ c. water

## Directions

Grind sesame seeds in a coffee grinder to make sesame flour and place in a bowl.

Add salt and lemon juice to flour and mix. Gradually add oil until desired consistency is achieved.

Stores in the fridge up to one month.

# Tangy Tomato Dressing

*Preparation:  Makes 1-2*
*10 Min.  Cups*

## Ingredients

- 2 c. tomatoes
- 1 tbsp. raw apple cider vinegar
- Himalayan crystal salt to taste
- white pepper to taste
- 1 c. dried tomato
- ¼ tsp. onion powder
- Pinch cayenne pepper
- ¼ tsp. paprika
- ¼ hot pepper

## Directions

Cut tomatoes and place in a blender, add raw apple cider vinegar, salt, pepper, and dried tomatoes.

Cut and seed the hot pepper and add it to the blender. Combine along with paprika, onion power, and cayenne pepper blend until smooth.

95

# Ranch Dressing

Preparation: 10 Min.  Makes 1-2 Cups

## Ingredients

- 1 c. almond sour cream (page 113)
- 2 tbsp. green onion, finely chopped
- 2 tsp. parsley, minced
- 2 tsp. onion, minced
- 2 tsp. celery seed
- ¼ tsp. paprika
- pinch cayenne pepper
- ¼ tsp. Himalayan crystal salt
- ¼ tsp. black pepper
- 1 tbsp. dill weed
- ½ c. water

## Directions

In a small bowl, combine almond sour cream, green onion, parsley, paprika, cayenne pepper, salt, pepper, and dill mixing well adding water as needed to achieve desired thickness. Refrigerate for at least 2 hours before serving.

## Variation

1) To have a winter dressing replace fresh onion, garlic, and parley with • ¼ tsp. onion powder • ¼ tsp. garlic powder 1 tsp. dried parsley. Continue making by following the reaming recipe.

2) For a Ranch Dressing Mix use dried ingredients and omit the sour cream. Store in an airtight container. To use combine with 1 cup of sour cream or nut mayo, mixing well and let stand for at least 20 minutes.

# *Strawberry Dressing*

Preparation: Makes 1-2
10 Min.          Cups

## Ingredients

- ¾ c. fresh strawberries
- 2 tbsp. lime juice
- 1 tsp. raw apple cider vinegar
- 4 tsp. coconut nectar
- 1 tsp. poppy seeds
- Himalayan crystal salt
- white pepper to taste

## Directions

Combine strawberries with lime juice, raw apple cider vinegar, and coconut nectar in a blender.

Add salt, pepper, and poppy seeds and blend until well combined.

## Variation

For cherry dressing omit strawberry juice and replace with cherry juice.

97

# *Italian Dressing*

Preparation: Makes ½
15 Min.       Cup

## Ingredients

- 3 tbsp. cold pressed olive oil
- 1 tsp. raw apple cider vinegar
- 1 tbsp. fresh parsley
- ¼ c. fresh lemon juice
- 1 cloves garlic
- 1 tbsp. fresh basil
- ¼ tsp. crushed red pepper
- ½ tbsp. fresh oregano

## Directions

Finely chop parsley, basil, garlic, and oregano then place in a bowl. To the spices combine oil, vinegar, lemon juice, and crushed red pepper whisk until well mixed.

You can also place ingredients in a jar with a lid and shake

## Note

For a winter dressing use ½ tsp. each of dried parsley, basil, oregano, and garlic powder or 1 tablespoon of Italian seasoning.

# Creamy Lemon Poppy Seed Dressing

Preparation: 5 Min.  Soaking: 10 Min  Makes 1-2 Cups

## Ingredients

- 1 c. cashews
- 2 lemons, juiced
- 2 tsp. organic lemon zest
- ½ tsp. mustard seed, ground
- 1 tsp. stevia leaves
- 1 tsp. Himalayan crystal salt
- 2 tbsp. poppy seeds
- ½ c. water

## Directions

Place cashews into a blender add lemon juice, organic lemon zest, ground mustard seed, stevia leaves, salt, and mix until smooth. Add water as needed until the desired constancy is achieved.

Remove dressing from blender and place in a bowl. Stir in poppy seeds and serve.

# Zucchini Carrot Bread Sticks

*Preparation:*   *Soaking:*   *Drying:*   *Makes 4-6*
*20 Min.*        *6-8 Hrs.*   *2-6 Hrs.*  *Servings*

## Ingredients

- 1 tbsp. chia or flaxseed, ground in coffee grinder
- ¾ c. cashews
- 2 tbsp. sesame seeds, ground
- 1 c. carrots, grated
- 2 c. zucchini, grated
- ¼ c. onion, chopped finely
- 1 cloves, garlic
- ¼ - ½ c. coconut flour
- 2 tbsp. nutritional yeast (optional)

## Directions

Combine ground chia or flax with 2 tablespoon water and set aside for 5 minutes.

In a blender, combine soaked seeds, cashews, sesame seeds, onion, garlic, and nutritional yeast until smooth. Add a dash of water, if needed, to make the mixture smoother.

Shred zucchini and carrots and place in a large bowl and combine with cashew mixture. Add coconut flour to the mix until well combined.

Spread mixture evenly on nonstick dehydrator sheet, and dry for 4 to 6 hours. Turnover and remove the nonstick sheet half way through drying.

When dried to desired texture (dry but not hard), cut into slices and serve.

---

### Fun Facts:

During WWII, the Royal Air Force was utilizing a new onboard radar system. To keep the true source under wraps, they started a rumor that fighters cat-like night vision was the result of a steady diet of carrots.

# Bread Sticks

Preparation:    Soaking:    Drying:    Makes 4-6
20 Min.    6-8 Hrs.    2-6 Hrs.    Servings

## Ingredients

- 1 c. gold flax, ground in a coffee grinder
- 2 c. buckwheat, sprouted
- 1 tsp. Himalayan crystal salt
- 1 c. dry buckwheat, ground in a coffee grinder

## Directions

Soak 2 cup of buckwheat overnight, drain water off and rinse buckwheat. In a food processor, combine buckwheat, ground flax, and salt. Mix until a thick dough is made

To make buckwheat flour, grind some dry buckwheat in a coffee grinder. Use buckwheat flour to thicken the dough if it is too sticky.

Sprinkle buckwheat flour on counter top. Knead dough in the buckwheat flour until it becomes pliable and easy to shape.

Form the dough into round sticks. Using buckwheat flour to keep it from sticking to the board or your hands. They should be narrow so they will dry.

If desired you can roll in sesame seeds. Place rounds on dehydrator tray and drive for about 1 hour and 100°F.

## Note

You can use raw coconut flour in place of buckwheat flour.

---

Fun Fact:

Buckwheat is not related to wheat, nor it is a cereal grain or grass. It is a relative of rhubarb and sorrel and its 'grain' is actually the dried fruit of the plant. When ground it behaves much like wheat and other grains.

---

# Veggie Crackers

| Preparation:<br>20 Min. | Soaking:<br>6-8 Hrs. | Drying:<br>6-10 Hrs. | Makes 4-6<br>Servings |
|---|---|---|---|

## Ingredients

- 1-2 cloves garlic
- 1 tomato
- 2 carrots, shredded (optional)
- 1 c. raw sunflower seeds, soaked 6-8 hours
- 1 c. raw pumpkin seeds, soaked 6-8 hours
- 1 red bell pepper, finely chopped
- 1 onion, finely chopped
- 3 celery stalks, chopped
- 1 tsp. caraway seeds
- 1 tsp. Himalayan crystal salt
- 2 tbsp. cold pressed olive oil
- 3 tbsp. raw tahini

## Directions

Soak pumpkin and sunflower seeds overnight. drain water and place seeds into food processor. Combine seeds and carrots in food processor until finely chopped.

Add tomato, garlic, bell pepper, onion, celery, tahini, olive oil, and salt and blend until everything is well incorporated.

Spread onto a nonstick dehydrator sheet a quarter of an inch thick. Lightly score the crackers and place in a dehydrator at 100°F for about 4 hours.

Flip the crackers and carefully remove the nonstick dehydrator sheet. Continue drying until desired crispness is obtained.

# Zucchini Crackers

Preparation: 40 Min.    Soaking: 6-8 Hrs.    Drying: 4-8 Hrs.    Makes 4-6 Servings

## Ingredients

- 1 c. raw sunflower seed, soaked
- 1 c. raw pumpkin seeds, soaked
- 2 carrots, shredded
- 1 red bell pepper, finely chopped
- 1 onion, finely chopped
- 3 celery stocks, chopped
- 1 medium zucchini, finely shredded
- 1-2 cloves garlic
- 1 tomato
- 1 tsp. caraway seeds
- 1 tsp. coriander seed
- 1 tsp. Himalayan crystal salt

## Directions

Cover sunflower and pumpkin seeds with water and soak 6-10 hours, drain water off and place in a food processor.

Add carrots and spices to the seed mixture and combine until finely mixed.

Add bell pepper, onion, celery, zucchini, garlic, and tomato to the food processor and mix.

Spread mixture on a nonstick dehydrator sheet until about ¼ inch thick. Dry at 100° F for about 4 hours. Flip and remove the nonstick dehydrator sheet.

Continue drying until desired crispness is obtained.

---

**Fun Fact:**

Zucchini has its ancestry in Central and South America and was introduced to Europe and the Mediterranean region by Christopher Columbus.

---

# Olive Jicama Crackers

Preparation:    Soaking:    Drying:    Makes 4-6
20 Min.    10-15 Min.    6-10 Hrs.    Servings

## Ingredients

- 1-2 cloves garlic
- 1 tomato
- 2 carrots, shredded (optional)
- 1 c. raw sunflower seeds, soaked 6-8 hours
- 1 c. raw pumpkin seeds, soaked 6-8 hours
- 1 red bell pepper, finely chopped
- 1 onion, finely chopped
- 3 celery stalks, chopped
- 1 tsp. caraway seeds
- 1 tsp. Himalayan crystal salt
- 2 tbsp. cold pressed olive oil
- 3 tbsp. raw tahini

## Directions

Soak walnuts, sunflowe seeds, and pumpkin seeds overnight. Drain water off and set aside.

Peel and grate jicama. Place in food processor with the onion. Blend until creamy, add walnuts, sunflower seeds, and pumpkin seeds and mix.

Add oil, salt, lemon, thyme, and ground flax seed and mix until smooth adding water as needed. Chop olives and gently mix them in the dough.

Spread the dough on a nonstick dehydrator sheet and dry at 100°F for about four hours. Flip crackers, remove the nonstick dehydrator sheet, and continue to dry for another 6-10 hours.

## Note

Use leftover jicama and olive soup if there is any. Add walnuts, sunflower seed, buckwheat and more olives then mix and dry.

---

**Fun Fact:**

Garlic is one of the oldest food flavorings that was discovered in ancient times.

# Basic Flax Crackers

Preparation: 15 Min.    Soaking: 10-15 Hrs.    Drying: 12-20 Hrs.    Makes 6-8 Servings

## Ingredients

- 1 c. flax seeds
- ¾ c. pure water
- ¼ tsp. Himalayan crystal salt

## Directions

Mix flax seeds with salt and or other spices. Pour water over the flax and stir well.

Let mixture soak at least about 15 minutes to overnight.

Spread mixture evenly on a nonstick dehydrator sheet. Dry for about 6 hours. Take the crackers out of dehydrator. Flip crackers and pull off the nonstick sheet. Continue drying for another 6-30 hours or until they are dry.

## Notes

If you do not like whole flaxseed grind them in a coffee grinder before adding the water.

Mix up the flavors by changing the spices and adding vegetables, such as corn for a **corn flax crackers**, or nuts and seed such as buckwheat, pumpkin seed etc.

An example for **Italian flaxseed crackers** add Italian spices and tomatoes. Make sure to chop the tomatoes well. Use your imagination and make the flax crackers you enjoy.

# Nadhirrah's Baykon

| Preparation: | Marinating: | Drying: | Makes 6-8 |
|---|---|---|---|
| 15 Min. | 2-24 Hrs. | 12-18 Hrs. | Servings |

## Ingredients

- 2 large Asian eggplants
- ¼ - ½ c. cold pressed olive oil
- 2 tbsp. raw apple cider vinegar
- 1 grapefruit, juiced
- 3 tbsp. Himalayan crystal salt

## Directions

Cut off top and bottom of the eggplant. While you can use any kind of eggplant, the long thin Asian eggplant will look more like bacon.

Using a mandolin, thinly sliced eggplant lengthwise. It should be long strips of thin eggplant.

Place a layer of sliced eggplant on the bottom of marinating pan. Sprinkle some salt over the top of that layer. Add another layer of sliced eggplant, more salt, and continue until the eggplant is all laid out.

Pour olive oil over the top of eggplant. Add the vinegar and grapefruit juice. If eggplant is not covered, add more oil and vinegar. If still not covered, use a little water.

Marinate for at least 2 hours and up to 24 hours. The eggplant may darken. That is okay, it is just oxidation.

Place marinated baykon in single layers on dehydrator trays.

Dehydrate about 18 hours. Baykon should be crispy when done.

# Curry Powder

Preparation: 15 Min. Makes 2 Ounces

## Ingredients

- 5 tsp. coriander seeds, ground
- 2 tsp. cumin seeds, ground
- ½ tsp. turmeric, ground
- ½ tsp. ginger, ground
- ½ tsp. mustard seed, ground
- ½ tsp. black pepper, ground
- ¼ tsp. fenugreek seeds, ground
- ¼ tsp. crushed red pepper flakes, ground

## Directions

If using whole spices grind them in a coffee grinder. Mix spices together. Store spice mixture in an airtight container in a dry place.

**Fun Fact:**

The earliest known curries are believed to have been created in Mesopotamia in around 1700 BC.

# Salsa

Preparation: 15 Min. Makes 4-6 Servings

## Ingredients

- 1 yellow bell pepper
- 1 red bell pepper, chopped
- 1 orange bell pepper
- 2 hot peppers, chopped
- 1 c. onion, chopped
- 4-5 fresh tomatoes
- 1 cloves garlic, minced
- 1 lime, juiced

## Directions

Wash and chop bell peppers, hot pepper, onion, garlic, lime juice and tomatoes place in a bowl and mix.

This can be done in a food processor and pulse but be careful because it can turn into soup easily.

# Sunflower Beans

Preparation: 15 Min.   Makes 4-6 Servings

## Ingredients

- 2 ½ c. sunflower seeds, soaked overnight
- ¼ c. cold pressed olive oil
- 3 ½ tsp. onion powder
- 1 tbsp. chili powder
- 2 tsp. cumin seed powder
- 1 tsp. Himalayan crystal salt
- 1 tbsp. raw apple cider vinegar
- ¼ c. onion, chopped
- 1 bell pepper (your choice color and combination)
- 1 hot pepper if desired.
- pure water if needed

## Directions

Soak sunflower seeds overnight. Drain off water and place seeds into food processor. Cut bell peppers, onion, and hot pepper then place in food processor with sunflower seeds. Add olive oil, spice, and vinegar combined until smooth adding only enough water to ensure consistency.

For people who are not used to raw foods, I recommend warming the beans in a dehydrator for an hour or so at 100°F.

# Cashew Cream

Preparation: 15 Min.   Makes 4-6 Servings

## Ingredients

- 2 c. cashews
- 1 ½c. pure water
- ½c. raw liquid sweetener
- ½ inch vanilla bean or 2 tsp. pure vanilla extract

## Directions

In a blender, combine cashew nuts, orange juice, agave nectar, and vanilla. Add just enough water to achieve a very creamy texture.

# Almond Mayo

Preparation:    Soaking:    Makes 6-8
10 Min.      8-12 Hrs.    Servings

## Ingredients

- 2 c. almonds, soaked overnight
- 3 tbsp. onion powder
- ½ c. cold pressed olive oil
- ¾ c. water
- 1-2 tbsp. Himalayan crystal salt
- ½ lemon, juiced

## Directions

Cover almonds with water, soak overnight and drain. While still wet peel the brown shell off each almond.

Place peeled almonds into a blender and add olive oil, onion powder, salt, and lemon juice.

Slowly blend adding enough water until a creamy, mayo consistency is achieved.

## Variations

For **cashew mayo** substitute cashew nuts for almonds. Cashews can become rubbery, so I usually do not soak them very long if at all.

This recipe can be used with almost any nut or seed you can think of. For example, hazelnut, pumpkin seeds, walnuts etc.

---

*Fun Fact:*

*There are two main types of almonds. One variety (Prunus amygdalus var. dulcis) produces sweet almonds, which are edible. The other variety (Prunus amygdalus var. amara) produces bitter almonds, which are used for almond oil.*

---

# Almond Sour Cream

Preparation: 15 Min.   Makes 4-6 Servings

## Ingredients

- 1 c. almonds, soaked
- 1 tsp. lemon juice
- 1 tbsp. raw apple cider vinegar
- ½ c. pure water as needed
- Himalayan crystal salt to taste

## Directions

Cover almonds with water and soak overnight drain water off. While skins are still wet, peel off the skin to create a white sour cream. If the skin remains, you will have a brown flaked sour cream.

In a blender, combine peeled almonds, lemon juice, raw apple cider vinegar, and salt. Purée until creamy adding water as needed.

Taste and adjust seasoning adding more lemon or vinegar if not sour enough.

---

# Ricotta Cheese Sauce

Preparation: 15 Min.   Makes 4-6 Servings

## Ingredients

- 1 c. macadamia nuts
- 2 cloves garlic
- 1 ½ tsp. Himalayan crystal salt
- 2 tsp. Italian seasoning
- ½ c. zucchini
- ½ c. water or more, as needed

## Directions

In a blender, purée macadamia nuts, garlic, zucchini, and spice until fluffy, while using as little water as possible to appear like cheese sauce.

# Almond Milk

Preparation:  Soaking:  Makes 6-8
5 Min.      8-12 Hrs.   Servings

## Ingredients

- 1 c. almonds, soaked overnight
- 2 c. pure water

## Directions

Cover almond with water and soak overnight, drain off the water while wet peel off the brown skin. Place almonds into a blender with 2 cups of pure fresh water. Blend for a minute or two.

Using a milk bag, (clean nylon sock, or cheesecloth) over a big bowl, pour contents of the blender into the bag.

Then squeeze out liquid for milk and sweeten milk if desired.

## Note

If you want use the almond pulp in another recipe such as almond mayo, cookies, crackers or bread.

## Variation

Nut milk may be made with any nut or seed that you can imagine such as **Brazil nuts, pumpkin seeds, sesame seeds** and **hazelnut** to name a few.

---

# Guacamole

Preparation:  Makes 4-6
15 Min.      Servings

## Ingredients

- ¼ c. mayo (page 112)
- 1-2 large avocados, pitted
- Himalayan crystal salt to taste

## Directions

Make mayo and set aside.

Remove avocado from the shell and place on a plate, add mayo and salt and mix with a fork.

# Spicy Nut Cheese

*Preparation:* *Soaking:* *Makes 6-8*
*15 Min.* *8-12 Hrs.* *Servings*

## Ingredients

- 2 c. almonds, soaked overnight
- ½ c. lemon juice
- ½ tsp. Himalayan crystal salt
- 1 tsp. fresh dill
- ½ c. green onion, chopped
- 1 red bell pepper, diced
- 1 chili pepper
- ½ c. dried tomatoes

## Directions

Cover almonds with water and soak overnight, then drain.

In a small bowl, cover dried tomatoes in water let soak for 30 min. Then drain and save tomato water for later use if needed (**don't** use the almond water). Fresh tomatoes may also be used in place of dried.

In a food processor, place almonds, lemon juice, salt, dill, green onion, red bell pepper, and chili pepper and combine until well mixed. Add dried tomatoes and blend until incorporated. Chill and serve.

## Note

**Serving Suggestion**

Serve on a flax cracker or other raw crackers or as dip with vegetables.

---

**Fun Fact:**

Cayenne pepper can be used for first aid when applied topically, cayenne pepper can help stop bleeding. The cayenne can either be sprinkled on the injury directly or diluted in water and soaked into a bandage.

---

# Vegan Feta Cheese

Preparation: 15 Min.   Soaking: 8-12 Hrs.   Fermenting: 8-18 Hrs.   Makes 6-8 Servings

## Ingredients

- 1 c. almonds, soaked
- ¼ c. fresh basil or thyme, oregano or other spice
- ¼ tsp. Himalayan crystal salt
- ½ c. rejuvalic

## Directions

Soak almonds overnight drain water off. Peel the brown skin off the almonds and place in a blender.

Pour Rejuvelac into a blender with almonds and salt. Blend at high speed, until it is a smooth.

Chop fresh basil and pulse into the cheese blender or mix by hand. If using blender make sure to only pulse otherwise you will have a green cheese.

Pour blender mixture into cheese cloth over a bowl or glass jar. Wrap the edges of the cloth, gently squeezing the liquid out. Hang cloth ball over the bowl, and leave for 8-12 hours. The longer it stands the stronger the flavor.

After fermentation time elapses, discard any liquid that has settle in the bowl or jar. Store extra cheese in the refrigerator; covered tightly.

## Variation

If you don't have Rejuvelac, you can use lemon, and a half a cup of water instead. If you use this method, however, the fermentation time may need to be extended to 12 -18 hours.

---

Fun Fact:

The almond is botanically a stone fruit related to cherry, plum, peach and apricot.

---

# Rawmesan

Preparation: Makes 6-8
15 Min.    Servings

## Ingredients

- ½ c. cashews
- ¼ c. raw, pumpkin seeds
- ½ tsp. Himalayan crystal salt
- ½ tsp. dill
- ½ tsp. nutritional yeast (optional)

## Directions

In a food processor, grind dry cashews and dry pumpkin seed into a powder. Add salt, dill, and nutritional yeast pulse a few more times. Rawmesan will keep about a month in the refrigerator.

---

# Sprouting

Sprouting happens when a seed germinates and begins to grow. Sprouts are considered living foods.

Energy is released and natural chemical changes occur so they are easier for the human body to assimilate. They are a convenient way to have fresh vegetables in any season and are easily grown in your home.

There are many methods of sprouting (jar, paper-towel, and tray). All sprouting is started by soaking seeds overnight, then placing the seeds in a jar or tray. Water seed two times a day. Drain water completely. The sprouts are ready when they start growing tails (1 to 6 days). Rinse and drain sprouts every three days after harvesting and store in the refrigerator, they keep up to a week.

Some sprouts can be grown into tender green plants (microgreens) such as peas, sunflower, and kale.

**Note:** Some bean sprouts such as pinto beans are very bitter when eaten raw. If using pinto beans, sprout them and then lightly steam them to remove bitterness.

Sprouts from nightshade family such as tomatoes, potatoes, peppers, and eggplants should not be eaten as the sprouts are toxic.

# Sprouting Rice

Wild rice is not really rice it is the seed of an aquatic grass. There are four species of wild rice. One native to Asia it is harvested as a vegetable. The other three are found in the Great Lakes region and harvested as grains.

Black wild rice will sprout, or bloom, by soaking it in water and changing water daily. This differs from other sprouts because rice grows in water.

Soak 1-2 cups of rice in water overnight. Drain and rinse and add fresh water. Rinse rice every day keeping rice covered in water 2-6 days (the length of sprouting time may vary based on climactic factors). Rice is ready to eat when it is soft and easy to chew, some wild black rice will split down the middle.

Brown rice can be sprouted but does not taste very good in my opinion. White rice will not sprout as the germ has been removed.

Note: quinoa will sprout like wild rice in water.

# Drying Nuts & Seeds

After soaking nuts and seeds to release the enzyme inhibitors, I like to dehydrate ones I am not using in a recipe right away. Once nuts are soaked, they will spoil. By drying them, they keep for a longer time and they are ready to use when needed. Dehydrate them at 100° F for about 18 hours.

> **Fun Fact:**
> An enzyme inhibitor is a molecule that binds to enzymes and decreases their activity. They are nature's way of preserving and making nuts, seeds, and grains last for a long period of time.

# Equipment

Having some essential equipment and knowledge will help make your preparation whole lot less stressful. For your convenience, I have provided suggested equipment.

• **Knives, Cutting Boards, Bowls, and Pans:** choose ones that you love.

• **Food processor:** is the 1st piece I would buy. It becomes your new best friend, and I use it almost every day. Choose one that has a lot of power.

• **Blender:** the most powerful blender you can afford. Even ones that do not have 1000 W of power will work for your food; it just may not be as creamy or fluffy as the more powerful blenders.

• **Dehydrator:** the brand does not really matter as long as it has a temperature control. I prefer the box type dehydrators with removable trays, this makes it easier to make pies, cakes, and casseroles.

• **Nonstick dehydrator sheets:** flexible sheets used with dehydrators.

• **Sprouting equipment:** I have the best success using the tray method. Get equipment that works the best for you.

• **Spiral slicer:** a vegetable slicer used to make vegetable noodles.

• **Juicer:** if you want to make nut butters and banana ice cream, you will need a masticating type juicer.

Don't worry about getting equipment all at one time. Start with what you will use the most. I already had knives, so the first tool I purchased was a food processor. I used my old blender until I could afford the one I wanted.

# Index

Kale Salad (page 64)

# About the Author

Kachina Choate, a long-time vegetarian, ironically didn't like vegetables. She stood up one day and said, "I'm tired of eating food that tastes like twigs, weeds and Styrofoam--there has to be a better way."

Since then she has been creating and serving healthy food to her unsuspecting friends who--when they find out say; "I can't believe I ate something healthy... and liked it!"

She is the author of In the Season Thereof, 101 ½ Raw Zucchinis and What to do With Them, Pumpkins Do Grow on Trees, Thriving on Plant Based Food Storage and Kachina Summer Bear Recipe Card Collection.

She began her natural, unprocessed, raw food journey in 2002, and as a result has recovered from depression and kicked a pernicious sugar addiction. She loves to travel and teach healthy food that tastes good.

She started Summer Bear Life Balance Education, a non-profit organization to help people achieve health and a balanced life.

Website: SummerBear.org; Facebook/ SummerBearLifeBalance; Instagram: summer_bear_org

Pinterest: dollkachina/raw-food-wfpb-food-storage-by- summerbearorg dollkachina/kachina-summer-bears-raw-foods